About the Author

Kavaljit Singh is co-ordinator of the Public Interest Research Group (PIRG) in New Delhi and the founder of Madhyam Books, a new publishing house committed to publishing on issues of current concern. He has written extensively on the question of foreign investment in journals and newspapers in India and abroad. His previous books include *TNCs and India* (with Jed Greer, PIRG, 1995) and *The Reality of Foreign Investments* (Madhyam Books, 1997). He is currently preparing a new book on the transnationalisation of production in the global economy.

D0107848

What the Critics say

'A very useful critical introduction to the workings, threats and possibilities of control of the global financial system. Highly recommended.' — *Professor Ed Herman*

'This book is exactly what was needed... A real citizen's guide.' — *Samir Amin*

'Don't be passively globalised: this book explains where you fit in the globalisers' plans and points towards new forms of resistance.' — *Susan George*

'Strongly recommended for all who are not familiar with economic jargon.' — *Economic and Political Weekly*

'Lucid... With minimal use of jargon... Singh achieves his objective: producing a useful layman's guide to the complex world of global finance.' — *Intelligent Investor*

'This accessible survey of a widely debated topic is recommended for general readers [and] students.' — *Choice*

'Although written for outsiders, this book should prove useful to the many ... denizens of financial institutions.' — *Investment Adviser*

'A sorely needed antidote to the hype about the benefits of globalisation... Does a superb job of explaining the nature of the problem and showing how obvious the solution could be.' — *Labour Left Briefing*

'It must be read by everyone who has to do with government policy on liberalisation and globalisation of financial sector policies and activities.' — *The Hindu*

'The book justifies the author's claim that it can be a tool to understand the complex issues and his hope that it will help in wider citizen participation in popular campaigns to reform and regulate the global finance capital.' — *Mainstream*

THE GLOBALISATION OF FINANCE:
A CITIZEN'S GUIDE

Kavaljit Singh

Zed Books Ltd
LONDON & NEW YORK

IPSR Books
CAPE TOWN

HG 3881
. S 537
1999

The *Globalisation of Finance: A Citizen's Guide* was published by
Zed Books Ltd, 7 Cynthia Street, London, N1 9JF and Room
400, 175 Fifth Avenue, New York, NY 10010, USA in 1999.

Distributed in the USA exclusively by St Martin's Press, Inc.,
175 Fifth Avenue, New York, NY 10010, USA.

ISBN 1 85649 691 0 (hb)
ISBN 1 85649 692 9 (pb)

Second impression, 2000
Copyright © Kavaljit Singh 1999

Published in Southern Africa by IPSR Books, Community
House, 41 Salt River Road, Salt River 7925, Cape Town,
South Africa
ISBN 0 9584224 7 8 (hb)
ISBN 0 9584224 8 6 (pb)

Published in South Asia in 1998 by Madhyam Books, 142
Maitri Apartments, Plot No. 28, Patparganj, Delhi - 110092.

ISBN 81-86816-08-9 (pb)

Printed and bound in Malaysia
Cover design by Andrew Corbett

A catalogue record for this book is available from the British
Library.

Library of Congress Cataloging-in-Publication Data
Singh, Kavaljit
    The globalisation of finance: a citizen's guide / Kavaljit Singh.
        p.   cm.
    Includes bibliographical references and index.
    ISBN 1-85649-691-0 hb and 1-85649-692-9 pb
    1. International finance.   2. Capital movements.   I. Title.
HG3881.S537   1998
332'.042–dc21   98-44116
                                                               CIP

Contents

JUL 3 0 2001

List of Boxes

List of Tables

Acronyms

ADB	Asian Development Bank
ADR	American Depository Receipt
APEC	Asia-Pacific Economic Cooperation
ASEAN	Association of Southeast Asian Nations
BIS	Bank for International Settlements
CAC	Capital Account Convertibility
EC	European Community
ECB	External Commercial Borrowing
EMS	European Monetary System
ERM	Exchange Rate Mechanism
EU	European Union
FDI	Foreign direct investment
FII	Foreign institutional investor
FOREX	Foreign Exchange
G-7	Group of seven highly industrialised countries
GATT	General Agreement on Tariffs and Trade
GDP	Gross domestic product
GDR	Global Depository Receipt
GNP	Gross national product
GSP	Generalised system of preferences
HIPCs	Highly indebted poor countries
IFC	International Finance Corporation
IFIs	International financial institutions
IMF	International Monetary Fund
IOSCO	International Organisation of Securities Commissions
MIGA	Multilateral Investment Guarantee Agency
NAFTA	North American Free Trade Agreement
NGO	Non-governmental organisation
OECD	Organisation of Economic Cooperation and Development

OPEC	Organisation of the Petroleum Exporting Countries
PI	Portfolio investment
RBI	Reserve Bank of India
SEBI	Securities and Exchange Board of India
SET	Stock Exchange of Thailand
TNC	Transnational corporation
UNCTAD	United Nations Conference on Trade and Development
VAT	Value-added tax
WTO	World Trade Organisation

Data Notes

Lakh is 1,00,000.

Million is 10,000,00.

Crore is 1,00,00,000.

Billion is 1,000 million.

Trillion is 1,000 billion.

Dollars are U.S. dollars unless otherwise specified.

1 U.S. Dollar = 39 Indian Rupees (1998).

Acknowledgements

I would like to express my thanks to all those people who provided support in bringing out this guide. In particular, I am indebted to Alex Wilks of Bretton Woods Project; Dalip S. Swamy; Jan Joost Teunissen of FONDAD; Marcia Caroll of Multinationals Resource Center; Mary Purcell of Equipo Pueblo; Michel van Voorst and Ted van Hees of EURODAD; Srisuwan Noi; Suntaree Kiatiprajuk of TDSC; and the library staff of the IMF and World Bank offices in New Delhi for providing me a number of research papers, publications, background materials and clippings. Thanks are also due to Deepak Nayyar; Equipo Pueblo; Forum of the Poor; Michel Chossudovsky; Multinational Monitor; Shripad Dharmadhikary; The Development GAP; Walden Bello; and many others whose writings and materials I have drawn upon in the preparation of this guide. Dalip S. Swamy and Edward S. Herman went through some chapters of the guide and provided valuable comments. Finally, the work would not have been completed in a short time without the editorial support of Pranjali Bandhu and computer typesetting by Ranjeet Thakur. However, the author remains responsible for any errors or flaws.

Preface

"I understand the globalisation of capital in production, but I don't understand the globalisation of capital as finance... I also find it extremely difficult to follow the financial terms and even financial pages of a newspaper...," a leading social activist involved in anti-TNCs campaigns in India told me last year, while discussing the Southeast Asian currency crisis. Her impressions are echoed by a number of other social activists and groups in India and elsewhere with whom I have had the opportunities to interact. Very few will disagree with the fact that in recent years there has been a significant trend of globalisation of capital in the form of finance rather than in production. Given the fact that there is hardly any book or other publication available which is written for non-specialist readers, I have taken the initiative to bring out a popular guide on this important theme. In fact, this guide is in continuation with an earlier publication that deals with FDI-related financial flows, especially in the Indian context, *TNCs and India: An Activists' Guide to Research and Campaign on Transnational Corporations* (with Jed Greer, PIRG, 1995).

This book aims at providing a simple guide to understand the language and world of finance. Part I introduces the concepts and aspects of global finance, while Part II deals with the recent experiences of developing countries with global finance capital. India's experience with such financial flows is also discussed here. The concluding section looks into the economic and political implications as well as the need for regulation and control of such flows. Finally, some campaign tools and strategies as well as information sources for further research and action are also provided for the interested readers.

In the words of Noam Chomsky, "Books can be either mere entertainment or useful tools in changing the world." This guide is intended as a tool to understand the complex set of issues related to globalisation of finance and its consequences. I further hope that it will serve as a catalysing factor for wider citizen participation in campaigns launched by many NGOs, labour unions and political groups.

Kavaljit Singh

To Mom, Fabby and Ishu

PART I

Global Finance: An Introduction

In this section, the reader is introduced to the concepts underlying the complex historical process of the globalisation of finance.

Chapter 1 outlines the evolution of the globalisation process which began in the mid-19th century. The linkages of the present phase of globalisation with the earlier one are traced out.

Chapter 2 describes the extent of global financial flows with specific reference to developing countries. It also deals with the major international as well as regional trends in financial flows and the contributory factors behind them.

Chapter 3 presents an overview of the growing role of institutional investors in the global financial markets.

Chapter 4 explains financial instruments, such as pension funds, mutual funds, bonds, etc., which now constitute an important component of global finance.

1

Globalisation: A New Phenomenon?

GLOBALISATION can be described as the process which involves growing economic 'interdependence' of countries worldwide. Many analysts are of the opinion that economic interdependence among the nations is not a new phenomenon, as popularly perceived. In fact, the present phase of globalisation is, in many ways, similar to the process of economic integration among nations, which began in the mid-1800s and ended with World War I. During that period artificial barriers to economic exchange among countries were few; and as a result, the flow of goods and capital across borders as well as migratory flows of people were large.

The present globalisation process is characterised by five major developments:

a) rapid growth in international financial transactions;

b) fast growth in trade, especially among TNCs;

c) surge in foreign direct investment, largely contributed by TNCs;

d) the emergence of global markets; and

e) the diffusion of technologies and ideas through rapid expansion of a globalised transportation and communication system.

The present phase of the globalisation process consists of two distinct phenomena - the globalisation of production and the globalisation of finance.

Globalisation of Production

The 1980s and 1990s have witnessed the rapid globalisation of the production process, facilitated by the structural adjustment programmes dictated by the World Bank and the IMF. This process has been further exacerbated by the multilateral agreements enforced by the GATT (now WTO). The driving force behind the globalisation of production are the TNCs. Faced with stagnant demand and sharp rise in production costs in home countries, the TNCs are shifting their production bases to developing countries where the domestic markets of goods and services are growing and the production costs are much lower, as raw materials and labour are very cheap. Given the fact that developing countries are now increasingly opening up their economies to transnational capital, this process has got further impetus. The globalisation of production has been made further possible by recent technological changes and reductions in transport and communications costs.

The growth of regional economic blocs (e.g. EU and NAFTA) in recent years has raised the question whether the current trend is towards regionalisation or globalisation. Financial flows and trade movements may have a regional bias and economic blocs discriminate the reduction of barriers only for member countries, yet the terms on which regionalisation is taking place remain global. For instance, competitive standards are global; tariff levels and trading rules are established globally; capital is raised in global markets; technology has global standards; and communication and information systems are globally based.

Globalisation of Finance

The process of globalisation of finance has assumed greater significance

Box 1.1

Globalisation: Old and New

Globalisation is nothing new. In many ways, the world economy in the late 20th century resembles the world economy in the late 19th century. The fundamental attribute of globalisation, then and now, is the increasing degree of openness in most countries. The openness is not simply confined to trade flows, investment flows and financial flows. It also extends to flows of services, technology, information, ideas and persons across national boundaries. There can be no doubt, however, that trade, investment and finance constitute the cutting edge of globalisation. The past two decades have witnessed an explosive growth in international finance. So much so that, in terms of magnitudes, trade and investment are now dwarfed by finance.

The four decades from 1870 to 1913 were the age of *laissez faire*. There were almost no restrictions on the movement of goods, capital and labour across national boundaries. Government intervention in economic activity was minimal. This first phase of globalisation coincided with what Hobsbawm (1987) has described as 'the age of empire,' when Britain more or less ruled the world. The second phase of globalisation, beginning in the early 1970s, coincided with the political dominance of the United States as the superpower. This political dominance has grown stronger with the collapse of communism and the triumph of capitalism, which has been described by another contemporary historian Fukuyama (1989) as 'the end of history.' It would seem that, in both phases, globalisation required a dominant economic power with a national currency that was, and is, acceptable as international money.

During the period from 1870 to 1913, an overwhelming proportion of international trade was constituted by inter-sectoral trade, where primary commodities were exchanged for manufactured goods. During the period 1970-1990, intra-industry trade in manufactures, based on scale economies and product differentiation, constituted an increasing proportion of international trade. During the present phase of globalisation, an increasing proportion of international trade is intra-firm trade, across national boundaries but between affiliates of the same firm.

In 1914, the stock of long-term foreign investment in the world

contd. on next page

economy was distributed as follows: 55 percent in the industrialised world (30 percent in Europe, 25 percent in the United States) and 45 percent in the underdeveloped world (20 percent in Latin America and 25 percent in Asia and Africa). In 1992, the stock of direct foreign investment in the world economy was distributed in a far more uneven manner: 78 percent in the industrialised countries and 22 percent in the developing countries. During the 1980s, industrialised countries absorbed 80 percent of the inflows of direct foreign investment in the world economy, whereas developing countries received only 20 percent.

The fundamental difference between the two phases of globalisation is in the sphere of labour flows. In the late 19th century, there were no restrictions on the mobility of people across national boundaries. Immigrants were granted citizenship with ease. Between 1870 and 1914, international labour migration was enormous. Since then, however, international migration has been reduced to a trickle because of draconian immigration laws and restrictive consular practices. The present phase of globalisation has found substitutes for labour mobility in the form of trade flows and investment flows. For one, industrialised countries now import manufactured goods that embody scarce labour. For another, industrialised countries export capital which employs scarce labour abroad to provide such goods.

The advent of international capital has meant significant political adjustments in the contemporary world. It has induced a strategic withdrawal on the part of the nation-state in some important spheres. Thus, nation-states are not the key players that they were in late 19th century during the first incarnation of globalisation. They remain the main political players but are no longer the main economic players. The process of globalisation has been uneven over time and across space. The inequalities and the asymmetrics implicit in the process, which led to uneven development in the late 19th century, mostly for political reasons, are bound to create uneven development in the late 20th century, mostly for economic reasons.

Deepak Nayyar

Excerpted from the author's presidential speech at the 78th annual conference of the Indian Economic Association in Chandigarh in December 1995.

and power than that of production, especially in recent years. The volume and mobility of global finance capital has surprised many observers. In 1986, about $188 billion passed through the hands of currency traders in New York, London and Tokyo everyday. By 1995 the daily turnover reached almost $1.2 trillion.

Historically, most trading in foreign exchange was the result of international trade, as buyers and sellers of foreign goods and services needed another currency to settle their transactions. But now, the trade in currency has very little to do with international trade, which accounts for just two percent of the global currency movements. Thus, the present process of globalisation of finance is no longer complementary to international trade and investment, but has gained a life of its own. In the current phase, financial flows are rarely associated with the flows of real resources and long-term productive investments. These flows are largely liquid and are attracted by short-term speculative gains, and can leave the country as quickly as they came. Besides currency trade, new financial instruments, such as bonds, mutual funds, GDRs and derivatives, have emerged in the recent past which have further contributed in the globalisation of finance. Let us briefly look into its history.

Table 1.1

Foreign Exchange Trading
(In billions of U.S. dollars and in percent)

	1986	1989	1992	1995
Global estimated turnover[1]	188	590	820	1190
As a ratio of:				
World exports of goods and services	7.4	15.8	17.4	19.1
Total reserves minus gold (all countries)	36.7	75.9	86.0	84.3

Sources: Bank for International Settlements; and International Monetary Fund.
[1] Daily average turnover, on spot, outright forward, and foreign exchange swap transactions, adjusted for local and cross-border double counting and for estimated gaps in reporting. Figures are based on surveys of activities in the three largest exchange market centres (London, New York, and Tokyo) in 1986, and markets in 21 countries in 1989 and 26 countries in 1992 and 1995. The London, New York, and Tokyo markets accounted for 57 percent of global turnover in 1989, 54 percent in 1992, and 56 percent in 1995.

In the 50 years before the First World War of 1914-1918, there was a massive flow of capital from the West European countries to the developing economies as then private capital could move without any

The Money Business

The origin of money began when people start trading the goods they had for the goods they wanted. Initially the barter system was commonly used but as the trade increased, money came into use. With money, buyers and sellers agreed to have an acceptable form of payment between themselves as well as in the wider trade circles.

Over the years, different forms of products have been considered money as a form of payment, such as salt in China, tobacco in Solomon Islands, and elephant hair in Africa. As early as 2500 B.C. metals such as gold and silver were used as money in Egypt. Later on, coins were used as money.

Paper money was perhaps first used in 1282, when Kublai Khan issued paper notes made of mulberry bark bearing his seal and his treasurers' signatures. The yuan, issued in China by the Ming dynasty between 1368 and 1399, is the oldest surviving paper money. Sao, the first paper money

in Vietnam, was issued in 1396. On the other hand, paper money was not circulated widely in Europe or the Americas until the 18th century when France popularised it.

Nowadays, whenever people think of money, they first think of paper currency. But, paper money has seen many ups and downs as its value fluctuated with the changing economic and political conditions. For instance, in 1923, because of the economic upheaval following World War I, many German households burned mark notes in their kitchen as it was much cheaper to burn marks than to use them to buy firewood. In 1923, you needed 726,000,000 marks to buy what you had been able to get for one mark in 1918 in Germany.

Besides, there are now other forms of money - checks, electronic transfers and cards. Just as currency replaced barter, electronic money in the form of credit, debit and smart cards is increasingly replacing cash.

restrictions. Much of it flowed into bonds financing railways, roads and other infrastructure, and into long-term government borrowings. During this phase, the international financial system ran according to the rules of the classical gold standard. As there was an unconditional guarantee to convert paper money for gold at a fixed price, this system was successful. With the outbreak of World War I, the gold standard was suspended and capital and exchange controls were imposed. After the war, controls were removed and the reinstated gold standard was characterised by virtually free capital mobility. However, the gold exchange standard was not as credible or viable as the pre-war standard, and countries following macro-economic policies inconsistent with maintaining gold convertibility became subject to destabilising capital flows. With the onset of the Great Depression of the 1930s, many countries imposed strict capital controls in order to use monetary and

Box 1.3

Dollar, Dollar, Everywhere...

The word **Dollar** comes from a silver coin called the *Joachimsthaler*, minted in 1518 in the valley (thal) of St. Joachim in Bohemia. This coin was called the **Daalder** in Holland, the **Daler** in Scandinavia and the **Dollar** in England. Nowadays, nearly two dozen countries have their currencies named **Dollar**.

Antigua & Barbuda	
Australia	**Jamaica**
Bahamas	**Liberia**
Barbados	**Namibia**
Belize	**New Zealand**
Bermuda	**St. Kitts and Nevis**
Brunei	**St. Lucia**
Canada	**St. Vincent**
Cayman Islands	**Singapore**
Dominica	**Solomon Islands**
Fiji Islands	**Taiwan**
Grenada	**Trinidad & Tobago**
Guyana	**U.S.**
Hong Kong	**Zimbabwe**

Box 1.4

The World of Currency

A currency's value - what it is worth in relation to other currencies - depends on how attractive it is in the marketplace. If demand for the currency is high its price will increase relative to other currencies. However, changes in the political environment (e.g. war, civil unrest, etc.), or economic run-down due to high inflation and trade deficits can cause a stable currency to fall, as investors tend to convert their currencies into foreign currencies considered to be more stable. This raises the value of the foreign currency. World currencies are traded regularly in the global foreign exchange market. Although three currencies - U.S. dollar, German mark and Japanese yen - dominate the world's currency trade, the prospects of any one of these to become the sole international currency seem to be remote.

EUROCURRENCY Any major currency on deposit in banks outside the country of origin is known as Eurocurrency, such as Eurodollars or Euroyen. The money can earn interest, be used to make investments, settle transactions between trading partners, or be loaned. Eurocurrency is popular in part because it is useful in international trade, where bills have to be paid in a specific currency.

CURRENCY TRADING The trading goes on round the clock, throughout what's known as the global trading day, which begins when the New Zealand market opens and runs through the end of New York trading. Published rates are updated regularly. A good profit can be made within split seconds and on small differences in prices.

Currency trading is carried out in the following three different ways:

Spot Transactions In spot transactions, the trade occurs immediately and is settled within two days. Spot transactions take place in an over-the-counter market, rather than at a central location such as an exchange. Trading is handled on the telephone or electronically through a network controlled by banks or other corporations. Though they account for less than half of the total currency turnover, spot transactions are big money deals, with minimum trade of $1 million.

Forward Transactions and Swap Contracts Forward transactions and foreign exchange swaps are contracts to exchange currency at an agreed upon price at a future date.

fiscal policy to insulate themselves from deflation and depression.

Since World War II, the dominant trend has been towards an increasing internationalisation of economic activity, largely facilitated by the successive rounds of GATT and imposition of liberal policies on the developing countries by the World Bank and the IMF. In the initial stages of internationalisation of economic activity, the U.S. and its allies played a central role to immunise the developing countries against the threat of communism by providing substantial financial support in the form of official aid and market access. To a large extent, the internationalisation of capital flows was used to finance the growth of trade.

Under the Bretton Woods system of fixed exchange rates that was set up after the Second World War and lasted until the early 1970s, the international flow of capital was heavily controlled. For instance, a British investor could not easily buy American stocks or bonds. The bulk of external capital available to developing countries was from official sources, both bilateral and multilateral. Foreign direct investment in developing countries, other than for exploitation of natural resources, was low. Commercial bank lending and portfolio investment were nearly non-existent. By the early 1960s markets had found ways of getting around some of these controls through the growth of 'Euromarkets,' where banks located in one country could take deposits and make loans in the currencies of other countries. When the fixed exchange rate system broke down in the early 1970s, the developed countries began dismantling their capital controls which was largely motivated by competition among them to attract international financial business. Led by the U.S., other developed countries removed curbs on capital movements.

Private capital flows to developing countries first surged in the mid-1970s in the form of commercial bank lending, when global oil prices rose steeply during 1973-1974. This price increase led to a massive transfer of funds from consumers to oil producers and had complex consequences for international finance. Many oil producing countries preferred keeping surplus funds in Western banks, which then needed to find investment outlets for these funds. They turned to developing countries who were eager to borrow these funds to fill budget and balance of payments deficits. Net flows to developing countries from commercial banks reached their peak by the late 1970s. Thus, foreign debts of such countries increased six-fold, from $100 billion in 1973 to $600 billion in 1979.

During the 1980s, commercial bank lending declined as many developing countries were under heavy debt burdens. As a result, in many countries net flows on private lending turned negative. However, the total flows to developing countries recovered at the end of the 1980s, with FDI constituting a large portion. The share of global FDI going to developing countries rose from 12 percent in 1990 to 38 percent in 1995. This was largely facilitated by the removal of capital controls in developing countries in the late 1980s and early 1990s.

Thus, both political and economic events, such as the breakdown of the Bretton Woods system, the oil crisis and the debt crisis contributed to the present phase of globalisation.

2

Trends in Global Financial Flows

IN the past one decade there has been a significant change in the character of financial flows, especially in the context of developing countries. A recent study conducted by the World Bank provides the following information:

■ Private capital flows now dominate the total financial flows to developing countries. Out of $285 billion of total financial flows in 1996, private flows accounted for $244 billion, over 80 percent of the total flows. This is a five-fold increase since 1990.

■ Private capital flows are nearly five times the size of official flows. This increase is significant as just five years back official flows to developing countries were larger than the private flows. In 1990-94, official flows declined significantly from 29 percent of total flows in 1990 to 6 percent in 1994. However, official flows rose steeply during 1995 as assistance was extended to Mexico in the aftermath of the crisis. For the first time in the 1990s, total net official flows to emerging markets in 1996 turned negative.

■ In Africa alone, official flows continue to be the largest source of flows, and in 1996 accounted for over 40 percent of total flows.

■ Net private capital flows to developing countries in 1996 were six times greater than they were at the start of the decade.

■ There has been a change in the composition of private capital flows. FDI has now emerged as the most important component of private capital flows. In comparison with commercial bank lending, FDI and PI dominate in the private capital flows during the 1990s. FDI has been the largest component of net private flows since 1995, and accounted for 45 percent of total private flows in 1996. While PI was negligible during the 1970s and 1980s, it became sizeable in the early 1990s. PI represented the largest component of flows between 1992 and 1994, and contributed $31 billion to the rise in net flows between 1995-96. The big increases came from bond issuance and from equity investment in local stock markets. Bond issuance was up by $17 billion to $46 billion, while portfolio equity investment was up by $14 billion to $46 billion.

■ Developing countries are now an important destination for global private capital. Their share of global FDI flows is currently almost 40 percent, compared with 15 percent in 1990; and their share of global portfolio equity flows is now almost 30 percent, compared with around 2 percent before the start of the decade. Portfolio equity flows are estimated to have rebounded from $32 billion in 1995 to a record $46 billion in 1996. Equity flows declined during the first half of 1995 as a result of the Mexican peso crisis.

■ A significant amount of private capital flows is going to the private sector as compared to governments just a decade back. Borrowings by the public sector and governments now account for less than a fifth of total private flows.

■ Another important feature of the private capital flows is that these flows are highly concentrated, with the top 10 countries receiving nearly three-quarters of capital inflows during the 1990s.

■ Borrowings through commercial bank loans are also rising. They were $34 billion in 1996, an increase of $8 billion from 1995. The majority of borrowers of commercial bank lending belong to the private sector, accounting for nearly 60 percent of all new loans in both 1995 and 1996. A large amount of these borrowings have been taken by the private sector in Chile, China, Indonesia, Malaysia, Mexico, South Africa, Thailand and Turkey. Another important aspect of commercial bank lending is that nearly half of it is used to finance projects, particularly big infrastructural projects such as power projects. This lending to support infrastructural projects is likely to increase in the coming years due to expansion of guarantees by governments and multilateral institutions.

The Regional Trends

According to World Bank estimates, the surge in private flows is concentrated in only 18 developing countries, which together received

Table 2.1
Financial Flows to Developing Countries[1]
(in $ billion)

	1990	1992	1995	1996[2]
Official Development Finance	56.3	55.4	53.0	40.8
Grants	29.2	31.6	32.6	31.3
Loans	27.1	23.9	20.4	9.5
Total Private Flows	44.4	90.6	184.2	243.8
Debt	16.6	35.9	56.6	88.6
Commercial banks	3.0	12.5	26.5	34.2
Bonds	2.3	9.9	28.5	46.1
Others	11.3	13.5	1.7	8.3
Foreign direct investment	24.5	43.6	95.5	109.5
Portfolio equity flows	3.2	11.0	32.1	45.7
Total Flows	**100.6**	**146.0**	**237.2**	**284.6**

Source: *Global Development Finance,* World Bank, 1997.
Note: Low and middle-income developing countries are defined as those having 1995 per capita incomes of less than $765 (low) and $9,385 (middle), respectively.
[1] Aggregate net long-term resource flows.
[2] Preliminary.

over 90 percent of all private flows during the period 1990-94. The largest recipients of private flows were the following: China (24 percent), Mexico (12.4 percent), Korea (7.2 percent), the former Soviet republics (7.1 percent), Argentina (6.6 percent), Malaysia (6.0 percent), Portugal (5.7 percent), Brazil (4.7 percent), Thailand (4.0 percent), Turkey (3.3 percent), Venezuela (2.5 percent), Hungary (2.3 percent), Islamic Republic of Iran (2.2 percent), India, Chile, Indonesia, Philippines, and Poland (all between 1 and 2 percent).

The private capital flows are limited to Latin American and Asian countries, and to some extent to a few countries within East Europe. Flows to East Asia and the Pacific continued their upward trend, rising to about $27 billion in 1995 and to an estimated $36 billion in 1996. Equity flows (including more than $8 billion flowing directly into stock markets) accounted for more than half the total in 1995, and bond issuance increased strongly in 1996. However, this trend reversed in 1997. According to the recent estimates of the Institute for International Finance, the flows to the Asian region witnessed sharp decline in 1997 largely because of the Southeast Asian currency crisis and its aftermath. The five countries which have been most damaged by the crisis - Indonesia, Malaysia, South Korea, Thailand and the Philippines - had net private inflows of $93 billion. But, in 1997, the net inflows turned into an estimated outflow of $12 billion. The swing in the net supply of private capital was $105 billion in just one year, a total of 10 percent of the combined pre-crisis GDP of the five economies.

While Asia remained the largest recipient of capital flows till 1996, Latin America has experienced the sharpest increase in capital inflows, which increased from $53 billion in 1995 to $74 billion in 1996. A large part of this increase was contributed by equity flows through depository receipts and investments by institutional investors.

On the other hand, the recent surge in private capital flows has largely bypassed Sub-Saharan Africa (except South Africa). In fact, during the period 1990-96, Africa received negligible net portfolio flows. The danger of outward net transfers on FDI is most clearly illustrated by Sub-Saharan Africa. Here, profit remittances have exceeded net inflows of FDI in every year since 1984, generating a net transfer over the last decade in the order of $20 billion. But the region's small share masks significant differences among countries and the types of capital flows they receive.

Although rates of return on FDI are higher in Sub-Saharan Africa in comparison with other developing regions (for instance, during 1990-94, rates of return on FDI in the region averaged 24 to 30 percent, compared with 16 to 18 percent for all developing countries), nevertheless FDI has remained limited to a few countries such as Angola, Botswana,

Table 2.2

Net Private Capital Flows to Developing Countries
(in $ billion)

	1990	1992	1994	1996[1]
All Developing Countries	**44.4**	**90.6**	**161.3**	**243.8**
Sub-Saharan Africa	0.3	-0.3	5.2	11.8
East Asia and Pacific	19.3	36.9	71.0	108.7
South Asia	2.2	2.9	8.5	10.7
Europe and Central Asia	9.5	21.8	17.2	31.2
Latin America and Caribbean	12.5	28.7	53.6	74.3
Middle East and North Africa	0.6	0.5	5.8	6.9
Income Group				
Low-income countries	11.4	25.4	57.1	67.1
Middle-income countries	32.0	64.8	104.2	176.7
Top Five Country Destinations[2]				
Brazil	0.5	9.8	12.2	14.7
China	8.8	21.3	44.4	52.0
Indonesia	3.2	4.6	7.7	17.9
Malaysia	1.8	6.0	8.9	16.0
Mexico	8.2	9.2	20.7	28.1

Source: *Global Development Finance,* World Bank, 1997.
Note: Low and middle-income developing countries are defined as those having 1995 per capita incomes of less than $765 (low) and $9,385 (middle), respectively.
[1] Preliminary.
[2] Country ranking is based on cumulative 1990-95 private capital flows received. Private flows include commercial bank loans guaranteed by export credit agencies.

Box 2.1

FDI and PI: A Comparison

There are substantial differences between Foreign Direct Investment and Portfolio Investments. In the case of FDI, investors exercise control over the management, while in the case of PI, investors only provide finance capital, and are not involved in management control. The investors are also different. In the case of PI, the investor base consists of institutional investors. For instance, Merrill Lynch, Morgan Stanley and Fidelity Investments are involved in PI. While investors involved in FDI are TNCs, such as Shell, Enron, Coke, Nestle, etc.

Usually, PI tend to be short-term, ranging from a few weeks to a couple of years. These investments can move out of the country as quickly as they came in because it is easy for portfolio investors to liquidate their investments by selling the stocks. Therefore, these financial flows are also known as 'hot money' flows. On the other hand, FDI tends to have a long-term investment period as it involves capital equipment, factories, etc., which TNCs cannot easily liquidate. Otherwise, the 'sunk' costs will be too high.

Political stability is the single most important factor facilitating both FDI and PI flows. However, investors of PI are only motivated by the financial returns on their investments through capital gains and dividends. Therefore, they attach more importance to high disclosure standards and easy repatriation of capital. On the other hand, investors of FDI are more interested in the size and growth of market, labour and production costs and infrastructure. Such investors do not attach much importance to disclosure standards and ease of capital repatriation.

The PI flows are more volatile than FDI flows. In a recent study by UNCTAD, it was found that the total PI flows to emerging markets have fluctuated more widely than total FDI flows during the period 1986-1995. According to the study, PI flows were four times higher than FDI flows. This study found that in the five emerging markets of Malaysia, South Africa, Thailand, Turkey and Venezuela, the relative variance of PI flows is many times higher than that of FDI flows.

Ghana, Mozambique and Uganda. The reasons for this include civil unrest, political instability, small size of domestic markets and slower privatisation of public sector companies. These factors, to a large extent, are similarly considered to have acted as impediments in the flow of portfolio investments in the region.

Factors Behind Surge in Portfolio Investments

The recent surge in portfolio investments can be attributed to a combination of factors, both external and internal, some of which are discussed below:

Low International Interest Rates

Among the external factors, perhaps the most important one is the relatively low real rates of return available on investments in the major developed economies from where these investments originate. For the past many years, the interest rates are very low in the developed countries as compared to emerging markets. This prompts investors in the developed countries to seek alternative markets for their investments in developing countries where the returns are higher. The sudden reversal of portfolio investments in 1994 in response to small increase in the real interest rates in the U.S. suggests that such investments will continue to flow as long as the interest rates in the developed countries are relatively low.

Factors in Developed Countries

Apart from low interest rates, other recent developments within the highly industrialised countries have also contributed to the globalisation of financial markets. These developments include rapid deregulation of their financial markets and growing competition among them.

Foreign exchange markets were the first to globalise in the late 1970s, followed by bond markets in the 1980s, and equity markets in the 1990s. As the banks' funding costs have increased, it makes economic sense for borrowers, such as governments and large corporations, to raise funds directly from investors through the securities markets. Largely in response to market pressures, governments began to deregulate domestic financial markets by the mid-1980s. Japan, for example, relaxed regulations on the Samurai bond market in 1983, issued the first Shogun bond in 1985, and relaxed restrictions on the holdings of domestic and Euroyen commercial paper by non-residents in 1988. The United States eliminated its 30 percent withholding tax on foreigners' interest income in 1984, the same year that Germany stopped taxing foreign investors' income from bonds. Germany also allowed foreigners to buy federal bonds in the primary market in 1988 and, a year later, eased restrictions on deutsche mark bonds.

Secondly, over the last one decade, there has been an institutionalisation of savings in the developed countries which provides large amounts of capital for investments. This has been further strengthened by the emergence of institutional investors who are both willing and able to invest internationally. With their help investors are assured of higher returns and risk diversification through investments in global markets. For instance, international investments by pension funds alone increased from $302 billion in 1989 to $790 billion in 1994.

Thirdly, the investor base has also grown in recent years with the decline of commercial banks and growth of mutual and pension funds. In the coming years, an increased growth of international investments by these instruments is likely to be witnessed because there has been deregulation of pension fund investments and privatisation of pension schemes.

Box 2.2

Stock Trading round the Clock

Stock trading goes on nearly 24 hours a day, on dozens of different exchanges in different countries in different time zones. As the trading ends in one city, activity shifts to a market in another city. Before the New York markets close, for instance, trading begins in Wellington; and two hours after Tokyo closes, London markets open. With two and a half hours to go in London, trading resumes in New York. The globalisation process has made it easier for institutional investors to trade simultaneously on different exchanges.

Major advances in the technological field, especially in communications and information, have also played a supportive role in the globalisation of financial markets. The influence of technological advances in overcoming the natural barriers of space and time has been most evident in the globalisation of financial markets. Nowadays 24-hour trading is possible, which was not the case a decade ago.

Growing Liberalisation of Financial Markets in Developing Countries

In the last ten years, the size and the structure of financial markets of developing countries have undergone rapid changes. The deregulation and globalisation of financial markets has been an important part of the structural adjustment programmes supported by the World Bank and the IMF. As a number of developing countries implemented adjustment programmes, they removed curbs and restrictions on foreign exchange transactions and international capital flows to facilitate the integration of domestic markets with global capital.

During 1991-93, 11 developing countries undertook full or extensive liberalisation of their exchange restrictions, 23 liberalised controls on FDI flows, 15 eased controls on portfolio inflows, and 5 eased restrictions on portfolio outflows. By the end of 1995, 35 developing countries had fully open capital accounts. The liberalisation of restrictions on portfolio capital has also translated into significant changes in the stock markets of developing countries. As recently as the beginning of 1991, only 26 percent of emerging stock markets could be categorised as having free entry for foreign investors, while 11 percent were closed to foreign investors. By the end of 1994, 58 percent of all stock markets had free entry for foreign investors, while only 2 percent remained closed. The number of countries that are classified as highly integrated increased from 2 in 1985-87 to 13 in 1992-94, whereas the number of countries classified as moderately integrated increased from 24 to 26 (see Annex A).

Portfolio investments get further attracted by the fact that developing countries are offering liberal tax concessions and benefits. In addition, a significant part of the surge in foreign equity financing has been associated with the privatisation of public sector companies in developing countries (for e.g. in Argentina), which is an important component of the structural adjustment programmes.

Apart from the structural adjustment programme, many international agreements also insist on the opening up of financial markets of developing countries. The recently concluded WTO agreement on financial services as well as the growing number of countries which have accepted the IMF's Article VIII obligations of convertibility of currencies for current account transactions is an indicator of this trend. For instance, the number of countries which have accepted the IMF's Article VIII has

Box 2.3

Capital Flight

It is very difficult to estimate the total amounts involved in capital flight as there is no accurate data available of these uncontrolled capital flows. However, attempts have been made by many economists and analysts to arrive at an estimate by analysing the errors and omissions entry in the annual balance of payments.

The issue of capital flight has traditionally been important in the context of Latin American countries where this phenomenon was very dominant. It has been estimated that the total stock of capital owned by Latin Americans outside the Southern Hemisphere reached between $210 billion and $250 billion in 1991, up by more than $100 billion from 1984. In Mexico alone the estimated increase between the mid-1980s and the early 1990s was over $40 billion - twice the official foreign exchange reserves held by that country in early 1994.

Recently, many economists in the Philippines have estimated that of every $100 which come to the country, $25 go out in capital flight. In Thailand, the errors and omissions category averaged over $700 million in unaccounted capital flows between 1987 and 1991, and $430 million in unaccounted outflows during 1992-93. Similar trends have been found in the case of Indonesia which witnessed outflows averaging nearly $1.5 billion for all but two years between 1987 and 1993.

increased sharply from 35 in 1970 (which was only 30 percent of the membership of the IMF) to 137 in early 1997 (76 percent of its membership). Besides, many of the recent international laws and agreements also contain provisions for the settlement of disputes between the investors and host countries through various mechanisms in which both parties can participate on an equal footing. This has further enhanced the confidence of the foreign investors in the developing countries.

These factors have not only facilitated financial flows from the developed countries to developing countries but, in recent years, have also contributed in the emergence of financial flows from developing countries (e.g. Mexico, Argentina, Thailand) to the rest of the world. Thus, the financial markets of the developing countries are now much more integrated with global finance than a decade back.

3

The Key Players

THE main players in the financial markets can be classified into four categories namely investors, both individual and institutional; companies; financial institutions, both domestic and international; and governments which act as borrowers and lenders and also regulate the markets. The recent phenomenal growth of institutional investors has surprised many observers. Since very little is known about the institutional investors, which now occupy a key position in the markets, let us look into their operations.

The driving force behind the financial flows to developing countries and elsewhere are the institutional investors which have emerged largely in the late 1980s and early 1990s. With the growing trend towards the institutionalisation of savings in industrial countries (from where the majority of funds originate), institutional investors now dominate the global financial world, especially the capital markets. In the U.S., for instance, institutional investors are now estimated to account for more than 49 percent of U.S. equities, compared with 16.5 percent three decades ago. With the U.S. based fund management companies dominating the business, the institutional investors manage and control assets worth billions of dollars.

By the end of 1996, out of the world's top ten fund managers, three belonged to the U.S., three to Switzerland, two to Japan and one each to Britain and France. As the home of the single largest pool of investible funds and as the most significant securities market in the world, the U.S. capital markets are of great significance to companies seeking foreign funds. In the case of debt, the U.S. is the only market which provides companies long-term funds at lower rates.

The U.S. institutional investors continue to roam the world in search for better profits and growth. According to the estimates of the IMF, U.S. portfolio investments are expanding so sharply that they now account for 12 percent of the country's total pension and mutual fund

Table 3.1
World's Top Fund Managers
(in $ billion)

Fund Managers	Country	Assets
United Bank of Switzerland[1]	Switzerland	920
Kampo[2]	Japan	798
Fidelity	U.S.	516
Axa	France	496
Barclays	Britain	385
Merrill/Mercury Asset Mgmt.	U.S.	382
Credit Suisse[3]	Switzerland	378
Prudential Insurance	U.S.	333
Nippon	Japan	332
Zurich[4]	Switzerland	312

[1] As of third quarter 1997.
[2] The Japanese Postal Insurance system.
[3] Including Winterthur.
[4] Includes Scudder, Kemper and Threadneadle Asset Management.
Source: Institutional Investor, UBS, SBC, *The Economist.*

assets. During 1991-96, U.S. investors have poured more than $330 billion into stocks and bonds all over the world.

Outside U.S., U.K. based institutions are the single largest investor group in international equities and a major investor in equity-linked instruments. The U.K. investors, including pension funds, insurance companies, unit investment trusts as well as foreign funds managed in the U.K., have large overseas investments. In the case of France, nearly 80 institutions are well known investors in international equities. Banks, insurance companies and pension funds control the majority of these funds. Most of the large funds have specific country fund managers for Europe, and specialists on the U.S., Far East and Australasia. In recent years, there has been increased interest by French institutions to invest in emerging markets.

Table 3.2

Top Mutual Fund Managers in U.S.
(by assets under management in $ billion as on August 31,1997)

Fidelity Investments	521.9
Vanguard Group	310.6
Capital Research & Management*	227.1
Merrill Lynch Asset Management	187.9
Franklin/Templeton & Mutual Series	165.2
Putnam Funds	161.0
Federated Investors	101.3
AIM/Invesco	93.9
Dreyfus Corp./Mellon Bank	88.5
Morgan Stanley, Dean Witter	87.0
Smith Barney	86.6
IDS Mutual Fund Group	85.0
SEI Financial Services	84.0
T. Rowe Price	82.4
Oppenheimer Funds/Mass Mutual	80.3

Does not include TIAA-CREF   *Part of Capital Group
Source: Investment Company Institute, in *The Economist*, October 25, 1997.

The large Swiss banks, life assurance companies and subsidiaries of overseas banks and investment houses dominate the Swiss institutions. The well developed private banking market in Switzerland provides access to a large number of investors. In Germany, the major commercial banks such as Dresdner Commerzbank, Deutsche and West LB and insurance companies, such as Allianz and Munich Re, dominate the market.

At the Asian level, Tokyo is the world's largest fund management centre with over U.S. $1 trillion under management. Close to two dozen institutions dominate the market. Apart from Tokyo, the other major fund management centres in Asia are Hong Kong and Singapore, with U.S. $80 billion and U.S. $30 billion under management respectively. Funds under management in Hong Kong represent foreign funds actively managed in Asia.

Growing Consolidation through Mergers and Acquisitions

Over the past one year, the fund management companies have undergone a swift consolidation process through mega-mergers and acquisitions. For instance, in December 1997, the merger of Swiss Bank Corporation (which was at the fifth position in the world) with Union Bank of Switzerland (at number three) has created the world's largest fund manager with assets totalling $920 billion. Similarly, the merger deal between Merrill Lynch, the U.S. investment bank, and Mercury Asset Management, the U.K.'s leading pension fund manager, has created a fund management company with $400 billion of assets. A year ago, both these companies were not in the list of the world's top ten fund management companies. Other recent deals include the $10.6 billion acquisition of Dean Witter Discover by Morgan Stanley and a $7.8 billion merger of two insurance groups, Axa and Union des Assurances de Paris. The world's top ten fund managers increased their assets under management from $3492 billion to $4220 billion in 1997, and a larger part of this increase resulted from the emergence of new entities through the merger and acquisition process.

Unable to compete with the global giants, the companies with relatively smaller funds under management are selling their businesses. For instance, LGT Asset Management - which only 18 months back bought Chancellor of the U.S. - recently decided to sell its asset management business of $65 billion. About six years back, there were hundreds of largely nation based fund management companies, but by the end of this decade only 20-25 global companies are estimated to exist.

In recent years, the rapid deregulation and globalisation of financial markets in the developing countries have led to the growing importance of institutional investors who have billions of dollars under management and are willing to invest in these countries. According to the estimates of the World Bank, institutional investors currently manage over $20

Table 3.3

Major International Fund Management/Bank Mergers *($bn)*

Deutsche Bank/Morgan Grenfell	Nov. '89	1.4
Franklin/Templeton	Aug. '92	0.9
SBC/Brinson Partners	Aug. '94	0.8
ING/Barings	Mar. '95	-1.4
Commerzbank/Jupiter Tyndall	April '95	0.3
Zurich Insurance/Kemper	Aprli '95	2.0
SBC/Warburg	May. '95	1.4
Dresdner/Kleinwort Benson	June '95	1.6
Barclays Bank/Wells Fargo Nikko	June '95	0.4
NatWest/Gartmore	Feb. '96	0.7
Morgan Stanley/Van Kampen American Capital	June '96	0.8
NatWest/Greenwich Capital Holdings	June '96	0.6
Franklin Templeton/Mutual Series	June '96	6.1
AXA/Union des Assurances de Paris	Nov. '96	7.8
Invesco/AIM Management Group	Nov. '96	1.6
Morgan Stanley/Dean Witter Discover	Feb. '97	10.0
Nations Bank/Montgomery Securities	July '97	1.2
J.P. Morgan/American Century	Aug. '97	0.9

Source: *The Economist,* October 25, 1997.

trillion in assets, of which only a small portion is invested in emerging markets. If institutional investors were to reallocate just 1 percent of their total assets under management towards the emerging markets, this shift would constitute a capital flow of $200 billion.

Among institutional investors, mutual funds are the leaders in equity investments. In 1986, there were 19 emerging market country funds and a few regional and global emerging market funds. By 1995 there were over 500 country funds and nearly 800 regional and global funds. The combined assets of all closed-and open-end emerging market funds increased from $1.9 billion in 1986 to $132 billion in the middle of 1996.

Similarly, total assets of pension funds at the global level are estimated to have increased from $4.3 trillion in 1989 to $7 trillion in 1994. At the same time, the share of international investment in their portfolios rose from around 7 percent in 1989 to 11 percent in 1994. Together, this has resulted in an increase in total international investments by pension funds from $302 billion in 1989 to $790 billion in 1994.

Overall, the combination of the growth in the assets held by institutional investors and their increasing global diversification has contributed in the surge of these funds to the developing countries.

4

Financial Instruments

TILL the early 1980s, the most dominant instrument of international finance was the syndicated bank loan. Since the commercial banks were flooded with inflows of short term funds and the demand for loans by developed country borrowers was depressed, most of the developing countries borrowers relied on this source. In the 1980s, private capital flows were largely in the form of bank lending to sovereign governments. However, the debt crisis led to sharp decline in the bank loans to developing countries in the late 1980s. Since then, the share of commercial bank lending in total financial flows to developing countries has significantly declined. Besides, new kinds of financial instruments have emerged which operate at the global level. Nowadays, the bulk of private capital flows is to the private sector and is increasingly taking place through financial instruments such as financial derivatives, International Bonds, Eurobonds, Global Depository Receipts (GDRs), mutual funds, pension funds, and equity investments.

Financial Derivatives

A major recent development in the globalisation of finance is the emergence of financial derivatives such as currencies and interest, stock and bond indexes, bonds and bills. A derivative product is a contract, the value of which depends on (i.e., is 'derived' from) the price of some underlying asset (e.g. an interest level or stock-market index). The three types of financial derivatives are forwards, futures and swaps. The key element in these derivatives is that one can buy and sell all the risk of an underlying asset without trading the asset itself. On the other hand, options are the rights (without obligation) to buy or sell a specific item - such as stocks or currency - for a pre-set price during a specified period of time. Futures and options are different from stocks, bonds and mutual funds because they are zero sum markets. In other words, for every dollar somebody makes, somebody else loses a dollar.

Trading of derivatives in raw minerals and goods dates back to the nineteenth century, while financial derivatives started in 1972 with currency trading. Stock-index futures trading began in 1982, and trading in interest-rate futures started in 1988. With the globalisation of financial derivatives, the value of outstanding derivatives contracts is estimated to be over $50 trillion. In the last two decades, the fastest growing global financial markets have been futures and swaps. Apart from currency markets, these are now the largest markets in the world. Like banking and securities, trading in financial derivatives is also distanceless and borderless. The trading is mostly carried out by global securities houses and a number of financial derivatives instruments are traded simultaneously on several exchanges in a round-the-world, round-the-clock market.

Speculators play an important role in the trading of financial derivatives. They keep buying and selling contracts depending on their perceptions of the movements of markets. Rumours play an important role in the decision making. Thus, derivatives markets tend to be very volatile and risk prone. With the globalisation of these markets, any major loss can have immediate world-wide repercussions. For instance, deficits of $1.3 billion accumulated by the Singapore based futures trader Nick Leeson triggered a transborder collapse of the Barings investment bank in 1995. Similar incidents have also occurred in the recent past, giving rise to apprehensions that financial derivatives trading could seriously jeopardise the global financial system.

International Bonds

Bonds can be described as loans through which the borrowers get the cash they need, while the lenders earn interest. As investments in stock markets tend to be risky, investors prefer bonds which are considered to be safe as they provide a fixed income through regular payment of interest, and the repayment of the principal amount is assured on the given maturity date.

The term of any bond is fixed at the time of its issue, and it can range from a year to 30 years, or even more. Usually, if the term of a bond is longer, the returns are likely to be higher.

Any corporation, or government, or multilateral institution (for e.g. World Bank and ADB) can issue bonds to raise resources for different purposes. For instance, corporations issue bonds to finance the growth and development of their businesses in order to earn more profits. As governments are supposed to provide basic amenities and infrastructure (e.g. roads, drinking water and education) and their revenues, quite often, are not enough to cover such expenses, they borrow money through bonds. Multilateral institutions, such as the World Bank and ADB, also issue bonds to raise funds internationally to finance infrastructure and other projects in developing countries.

In recent years, the composition of external financing of developing countries has changed due to the emergence of international bonds. These countries prefer raising funds through issuance of bonds rather than bank lending, which was the case in the 1980s. International bonds now constitute the single largest source of debt financing in developing countries. The international bonds include Eurobonds, sovereign bonds, regional bonds and so on. The total turnover of international bonds was estimated to be $5.3 trillion in 1996.

The largest single-tranche Eurobond of $6 billion was floated by Mexico in 1996. In November 1996, Russia placed a $1 billion issue - the largest ever debt sovereign issue. Recently, Enron Corporation has

Box 4.1

Bond Ratings

Bond ratings are carried out to inform the investors whether their investments in particular bonds are risky or not. At the global level, the best known services are Standard & Poor's Corp. and Moody's Investors Service Inc. These companies investigate the financial condition of a bond issuer as well as the macro-economic conditions of the economy. Rating companies rank all types of international bonds. For instance, the ADB debt is rated triple-A. These companies also rate countries to inform foreign investors about the prospects of investments in them.

In India, three agencies, namely, ICRA, CRISIL and CARE are involved in the ratings of bonds and other financial instruments.

Moody's	Standard & Poor's	Meaning
Aaa	AAA	Best quality, with the smallest risk; issuers exceptionally stable and dependable.
Aa	AA	High quality, with slightly higher degree of long-term risk.
A	A	High to medium quality, with many strong attributes, but somewhat vulnerable to changing economic conditions.
Baa	BBB	Medium quality, currently adequate but perhaps unreliable over long term.
Ba	BB	Some speculative element, with moderate security, but not well safeguarded.
B	B	Able to pay now but at risk of default in the future.
Caa	CCC	Poor quality, clear danger of default.
Ca	CC	Highly speculative quality, often in default.
C	C	Lowest-rated, poor prospects of repayment though may still be paying.
—	K	Interest payments are in default.

used bonds to finance its first power project outside the U.S..

Apart from Latin America, bond markets are growing in the Asia-Pacific region as well. For instance, Japan has the largest bond market in the region, followed by Australia and New Zealand. Hong Kong's bond market is also well developed, while markets in South Korea, Malaysia and Thailand are in the developing stage.

The important categories of bonds are described below:

Domestic Bonds These bonds are issued and sold within the country.

Overseas Bonds These bonds are issued in one country in its currency but sold in another country in the currency of that country. In fact, you can sometimes buy bonds issued in two countries at the same time and sold in a third currency.

Eurobonds These are standard international bonds with the following characteristics - the currency of the bond is not that of the place of issue, the issuers of the bonds are foreign to the place of issue, and the bonds are not sold in the capital markets of one country but are distributed worldwide. Eurobonds floated by the Indian companies are commonly referred to as Foreign Currency Convertible Bonds (FCCBs). FCCBs are basically equity linked debt securities, to be converted into equity or

---

Box 4.2

World Bank and ADB: Lenders or Borrowers?

In the eyes of the general public, the World Bank and the ADB are seen as generous lenders who lend money to third world countries to support developmental projects. In fact, both these institutions are borrowers too. The ADB, which has 56 countries as members, raises money through international debt offerings. For instance, in early 1998, the ADB launched a $ 387 million bond for the Hong Kong domestic market, the proceeds of which will be used to augment its lending resources.

Similarly, the World Bank raises money by issuing bonds to individuals, institutions and governments in more than 100 countries. The bonds are guaranteed by the governments of the 178 countries who are members of the Bank, and who technically 'own' it.

depository receipts after a specific period. Thus, a holder of FCCBs has the option of either converting it into equity (normally at a predetermined formula and even a predetermined exchange rate), or retaining the bond. The FCCBs carry a fixed rate of interest and can be marketed conveniently.

Yankee Bonds are issued by an overseas borrower for U.S. investors. They are payable in dollars and registered with the U.S. Securities and Exchange Commission.

Samurai Bonds are yen-denominated bonds issued in Japan by overseas governments or companies. The bonds can be settled only in Japan, though they may be dual-currency issues. That means the payment and the interest are in yen, but the redemption is in another currency, such as the dollar or the Australian dollar. In a reverse dual-currency issue, the payment and redemption are in yen, but the interest is paid in another currency.

Dragon Bonds These bonds are launched and priced in Asia for non-Japanese Asian investors.

Subordinated Bonds These bonds are repaid by the issuer when other loan obligations have been met.

Senior Bonds These bonds carry stronger claims.

Convertible Bonds These bonds give investors the option to convert, or change their corporate bonds into company stock, instead of getting a cash repayment. The terms are set at issue; they include the date when the conversion can be made, and how much stock each bond can be exchanged for.

Callable Bonds Callable bonds do not always run their full term. The issuer may call the bond and pay off the debt before the maturity date. Issuers may call a bond if interest rates drop and after paying their outstanding bonds, they can issue another bond at the lower rate. Sometimes only part of an issue is redeemed. These bonds are also known as *Redemption Bonds.*

Zero-Coupon Bonds Since coupon, in bond terminology, means interest, a zero coupon by definition pays out no interest while the loan is maturing. Instead, the interest accrues, or builds up, and is paid in a lump sum at maturity. Investors prefer zero-coupon bonds because they get them at deep discount, (i.e., at prices far lower than par value). When the bond matures, the accrued interest and the original investment add up to the bond's par value. Issuers prefer such bonds because they can continue to use the loan money without paying regular interest.

Inflation-Indexed Bonds In the U.S., and recently in India also, these bonds are being issued. The bonds protect investors from the negative impacts of inflation as these are linked with the inflation rate, and their value remains constant irrespective of inflation.

Investors generally prefer to invest in bonds which are issued in their own currency rather than in any foreign currency, which carries the risk of shifts in value due to depreciation and devaluation. In many countries, there are restrictions on the buying of domestic bonds. In

Table 4.1

International Bond Issues in 1997

Issuers	Number of Issues
Morgan Stanley	426
Merrill Lynch	380
Deutsche Morgan Grenfell	261
Nomura Securities	203
J.P. Morgan	189
Credit Suisse-First Boston	183
SBC Warburg Dillon Read	181
ABN-Amro Hoare Govett	162
Lehman Brothers	152
Union Bank of Switzerland	150
Goldman Sachs	132
Salomon Smith Barney	130
Banque Paribas	119
HSBC	99
Barclays de Zoete Wedd	88

Source: Capital DATA Bondware, in *The Economist*, January 17, 1998.

other countries, for instance, any buyer can purchase the bonds. It has been estimated that at the end of 1995 about 26 percent of all privately held treasury bonds were held by non-U.S. investors, nearly 7 percent by Japanese investors.

In 1997, the top 20 firms issued more than 4,600 international bonds, raising a total of $742 billion, up from $679 billion raised in 1996. Dollar-denominated bonds provided the biggest share of new issues - some 48 percent of the total in 1997, up from 40 percent a year earlier. American investment banks dominated the bond issuance business. Out of the top ten international issuers, five were American banks, two Swiss, two Dutch and one German. Merrill Lynch managed $57 billion of international bond issues, while Morgan Stanley finished second in value terms.

Mutual Funds

In simple terms, a mutual fund is a collection of stocks, bonds or other securities owned by a group of investors and managed by a professional

---

Box 4.3

What is Sensex?

The performance of any stock market - whether it is going up or down - is reported in an Index or Average. The Index or Average serves as an important tool for measuring the overall health of the stock market. In most countries, there is more than one Index.

The Index or Average is known by different names in different countries. For instance, one of the well known and most widely reported Index of Bombay Stock Exchange is **Sensitive Index** (popularly known as **Sensex**). Similarly, in other countries, the popular and widely reported Index are - **Nikkei** in Tokyo; **Hang Seng** in Hong Kong; **Composite** in Jakarta, Manila, Seoul and Kuala Lampur; **Dow Jones Industrial Average, Standard & Poor's 500 Index** and **Nasdaq Composite Index** in U.S.

At the international level, the World Stock Index (e.g. **Dow Jones World Stock Index**) measures the performance of the stock markets of major countries in the world.

investment company. Also known as *unit trusts*, these funds offer better returns to investors as the professional investment company keeps regular track of markets. Rather than investing individually, investors prefer putting their money into mutual funds through which they have more buying power. Mutual funds are created by investment companies (which are known as mutual fund companies or managers), brokerage houses and banks, which offer a whole range of funds to suit the investors' choice.

As many of these funds are global in nature and denominated in different currencies, one may find the U.S. based funds investing in the Asia-Pacific region, and Hong Kong-based funds investing in Latin America. Most funds diversify their holdings by buying a wide variety of investments which helps in offsetting losses from some investments by gains in other investments. In mid-1996, there were more than 36,000 funds available world-wide. These included more than 7,500 in the U.S., and thousands in Hong Kong, which is Asia's fund management capital. By 1994, pension funds, insurance companies, and mutual funds in the OECD countries had grown to $20 trillion.

It has been estimated by the World Bank that in 1996 $34 billion in external flows went directly to domestic stock markets of developing countries through pension funds, mutual funds, hedge funds,* and other investment vehicles. The big recipients are Latin American and Asian countries as well as the Czech Republic, Poland and Russia. The biggest mutual fund industry is based in the U.S., which has nearly $4.2 trillion in assets. According to the Investment Company Institute, around 15-20 percent of it comes from pension schemes funded through voluntary deductions from employees' pay and contributions by the employers. It has been estimated that nearly $21 billion are provided by these schemes to fund managers.

---

* International fund managers often use a practice called hedging. If a currency gains relative to others, investments denominated in other currencies have less value when converted into it. To protect against that, funds often hedge, or buy futures contracts, or a currency at a pre-set exchange rate. Some funds don't hedge at all, as seen in the case of the Southeast Asian crisis, where a large number of companies faced a severe crisis of repayments because of this.

So far, the international exposure of pension funds is lower than that of mutual funds, except in Japan and the U.S.. These funds hold about $70 billion of emerging market assets. Nonetheless, pension funds are fast becoming an important source of investments despite the fact that these are heavily regulated, less globalised and more oriented towards long-term investments. However, with the growing trend of privatisation of pension schemes in the developed countries, pension funds are likely to be a major force in the demand for portfolio equities from developing countries. As with mutual funds, most pension fund investments in emerging markets are in the form of portfolio equities.

Broadly, mutual funds can be divided into three main categories:

Stock Funds These are invested in stocks;

Bond Funds Like bonds, these funds provide regular income to investors; and

Money-Market Funds Quite similar to savings accounts in the bank. For every rupee you put in, you get a rupee back, plus the interest your money earns from the investments the fund makes. Since these funds are usually price-stable, some investors prefer them to stock or bond funds.

There are other types of funds, some of which are briefly described below:

Open-End Funds Under such funds, an investor can buy as many shares he/she wants. As investors put money into it, the fund grows.

Closed-End Funds Closed-end funds resemble stocks in the way they are traded. While these funds do invest in a variety of securities, they raise money only once, offer only a fixed number of shares and are traded on a stock exchange. The market price of a closed-end fund fluctuates in response to investor demand as well as to changes in the value of its holdings. These funds are also known as *Exchange Traded Funds* or *Over the Counter Funds.*

Global Funds These funds are invested in various stock or bond markets in the world. By spreading investments throughout the world, these funds can balance risk by owning securities in both volatile and stable markets.

Regional Funds These funds are concentrated in several countries of a particular geographical region, for instance, Thailand and Philippines in Southeast Asia, or Chile and Argentina in Latin America. Since countries in different geographical regions provide diverse returns on investments, these funds aim to capitalise on this diversity.

Country Funds These funds allow investors to concentrate their investments in a single overseas country, even countries whose markets are closed to non-resident individual investors. When a fund does well, other funds are set up for the same country by the fund companies. In recent years, many Indian funds have been created by the global fund companies. By buying stocks and bonds in a single country, investors can profit from the strength of an established economy. For this reason, country funds were very popular in Southeast Asian countries in the early 1990s.

Offshore Funds These funds are, quite often, based in tax havens in order to benefit from liberal tax regimes offered in such places.

Global Depository Receipts

The GDRs are negotiable instruments meant for raising equity in the international financial markets. They are created by overseas depository banks which are authorised by issuing companies to issue GDRs outside the country. They can be listed in any overseas stock exchange and may be purchased and transferred by non-residents in foreign currency. The cost of acquiring shares through the GDR route is cheaper because they are issued at a discount on the market price. A number of international equity offers, particularly from some Asian markets, have increasingly used GDRs, where legal restrictions and closed markets have prevented the free trading of equities. A company interested in issuing GDRs will issue shares to a foreign depository. The depository, in turn, issues GDRs to investors. ADRs remain the most preferred form of foreign equity investments by the U.S. investors.

The issuer issuing the shares has to pay dividends to the depository in the domestic currency. The depository has to then convert the domestic currency into foreign currency for onward payment to the receipt holders. In India, many companies have issued GDRs in recent years.

Other Financial Instruments

In recent years, new financial instruments to finance large infrastructure projects (e.g. power plants, toll roads, etc.) in developing countries have come up. These financial packages may have a combination of equity (both FDI and FPI) and debt (both bonds and loans). They can be financed by both private and official sources. Quite often, such projects are based on the principles of build-operate-transfer (BOT), or build-own-operate-transfer (BOOT), or build-own-operate (BOO).

Increasingly, such projects have sovereign guarantees from the governments as well as non-commercial guarantees from MIGA and other bodies. In many countries, including India, a number of projects financed through a combination of such instruments are coming up, especially in the large infrastructure projects. At the global level, an estimated $5 billion have been raised through these instruments to finance large infrastructure projects in developing countries.

Part II

Recent Financial Crises in Developing Countries: Experiences and Lessons

The 1990s saw a number of financial crises erupting in many developing countries, especially those which were touted as 'model economies' by the international financial institutions. Beginning with the Mexican crisis, the so-called 'Asian Tigers' were the next to be affected by the modus operandi of global finance capital.

Chapters in this part analyse the financial crisis in Mexico in 1994-95 and the Southeast Asian currency crisis in 1997. The impacts of these financial crises on the real economy and people are delineated. A critique of policy responses of governments and the politics of bailouts to deal with the financial crises is presented.

In this background, the wider implications of India's recent moves to open up its financial markets to global finance are discussed in the last chapter.

5

Collapse of a 'Model':
The Mexican Financial Crisis

The Origins

FOR many years, in the late 1980s and early 1990s, Mexico was touted as a 'model economy.' During this period major economic reforms were undertaken, with liberalisation and privatisation policies replacing the earlier model of state-led growth. Since these policies were initiated and implemented with the support of the World Bank and IMF, the Mexican case was hailed as a 'success story' by these institutions, which other Latin American countries were encouraged to emulate. As a fallout of these neo-liberal economic policies, foreign investors started investing heavily in Mexico and over $90 billion flowed into the country during 1990-93. Almost two-thirds of these investments were in the form of portfolio investments.

A number of external and internal factors were behind the massive upsurge in foreign investments in Mexico. The single major external factor was low interest rates in the U.S. combined with the recession there and in other countries, which prompted investors to invest in Mexico and elsewhere for bigger profits. The Brady Plan deal of 1989* and Mexico's entry into the NAFTA with the U.S. and Canada also enhanced the creditworthiness of Mexico in the eyes of foreign investors. The major internal factors encouraging foreign investments were higher GDP growth rate at an average of 3.1 percent per year between 1988 and 1994; a low inflation rate which declined from nearly 145 percent to a mere 6 percent;[1] and large-scale privatisation of state-owned enterprises.

Another significant reason behind the massive surge in foreign investments was the return of the funds that had flowed out from Mexico to the U.S. during the Mexican debt crisis in the eighties. Anticipating an improvement in economic conditions in Mexico in the 1990s, the wealthy Mexicans brought back these funds.[2]

The majority of these inflows were short-term and aimed at making quick profits through financial speculation on stocks and other securities in the financial markets of Mexico. Only a small portion of portfolio investments was used to create new physical assets, such as factories or machinery. Thus, the gains from the foreign investments were more illusory than real.

Moreover, with the increased availability of foreign funds and growing dependency on them, Mexico was confronted by a sharp fall in the domestic savings which came down from 22 percent of the GDP in 1988 to 16 percent in 1994. Secondly, Mexico used these funds to finance its burgeoning import consumption. Despite the fact that during this period the exports from Mexico also picked up, the import bill rose more rapidly, leading to a current account[†] deficit of nearly $30 billion, equivalent to 8 percent of the country's GDP in 1994. This rise in current account

---

* A scheme devised in 1989 by U.S. Secretary of the Treasury, Nicholas Brady, (with bank and government approval) providing debtor nations with three options for handling their debts: reduced principal, reduced interest rates, or new loans.

† Current account is a summary item in the balance of payments which measures the net of exports and imports of merchandise and services, investment income and payments, and government transactions.

Box 5.1

The Mexican Debt Crisis

In 1982, Mexico announced that it lacked funds to repay loans and stood on the verge of default. In the early 1980s, when the oil prices began to drop, Mexico faced an almost $6 billion drop in its oil revenues. Declining oil revenues coupled with growing external borrowings and an overvalued exchange rate (which encouraged imports and discouraged exports) led to the situation of default.

Mexico owed large sums to private banks in the U.S. and other Northern countries. For instance, it owed the Bank of America and Citibank roughly $3 billion each. Citibank's Mexican exposure equalled two-thirds of its net corporate assets.

Anticipating a crisis which would not only hurt Mexico but the U.S. based banks too, the U.S. government stepped in to provide emergency short-term financing so that Mexico could repay its debt. As part of the deal, the U.S. also provided $1 billion advance payment for discounted Mexican oil, as well as $1 billion in credits toward the purchase of surplus U.S. grain. Mexico subsequently entered into negotiations with the IMF and its private bank creditors, during which debt payments were suspended for 120 days. Ultimately, a new financing plan was prepared by the IMF which led to repayments over a longer time period. In return, Mexico agreed to follow a stabilisation plan designed by IMF officials which included devaluation of the peso, reduction in its budget deficit, cuts in food subsidies and a freeze on wages. As more and more countries started facing a debt crisis, the IMF assumed the central role by designing stabilisation and austerity programmes.

Despite this bailout, Mexico once again found itself approaching default, which led to another rescheduling agreement, and other measures such as debt-for-equity swaps were also taken up. Finally, in 1989 the Mexican government signed a plan with a committee of creditor banks.

Before the restructuring of its external debt, Mexico was a net exporter of capital. The reduction of external debt service and the growing investment opportunities created by adjustment policies made Mexico a favourite destination of foreign investment.

Box 5.2

Chronology of Mexican Crisis

1994

JANUARY 1:	Nafta goes into effect; Chiapas uprising.
MARCH:	PRI presidential candidate Luis Donaldo Colosio assassinated.
AUGUST:	Ernesto Zedillo elected president.
SEPTEMBER:	PRI general secretary Jose Francisco Ruiz Massieu assassinated.
NOVEMBER:	Concerns in market about Zedillo's ability to follow Salinas' policies and keep a stable currency start causing jitters; As of November 18 the *peso* is down 11 percent, and concern is growing about problem loans at banks.
NOVEMBER 30:	Cabinet appointed Guillermo Ortiz as communication and transportation minister and Jaime Serra Puche as finance minister.
DECEMBER 8:	Zedillo budget projects 4 percent increase in GDP in 1995.
DECEMBER 20-21:	Devaluation, followed by decision to let *peso* float.
DECEMBER 29:	Zedillo names Ortiz to replace Serra Puche. Markets praise the move. They were outraged that Serra let the *peso* float only days after he said he would not do so.

1995

JANUARY 2:	Zedillo announces austerity plan; markets say it's not tough enough.
MID-JANUARY:	Clinton fails to get Congress to pass Mexico aid package.
FEBRUARY 1:	IMF announces $17.8 billion standby credit for Mexico; it withdraws $7.8 billion immediately.
MID-FEBRUARY:	$3 billion loan from international banks falls through.
FEBRUARY 21:	U.S. and Mexico announce $20 billion aid package, with funds from the Treasury's Exchange Stabilisation Fund. Mexico pledges oil revenues as part of collateral.
MARCH 14:	Mexico draws $3 billion from U.S. package.

contd. on next page

MID-APRIL:	G-7 ministers bring up concept of a rescue fund for Mexico-like crises; several leading Republican senators object to the idea.
APRIL 19:	Mexico draws $3 billion from U.S. package.
MAY 19:	Mexico draws $2 billion from U.S. package.
MAY 31:	Zedillo presents national development plan for 1995-2000; meanwhile, his administration loosens the money supply a bit.
JUNE 21:	Mexico and IDB sign $1.25 billion loan agreement on March 9.
JUNE 23:	World Bank approves $1.5 billion loan to Mexico.
JUNE 30:	IMF releases remaining $10 billion of promised loan to Mexico, with $2 billion to be made available immediately.
JULY:	Mexico returns to the market with its $1.1 billion global bond issue; Draws $2 billion from IMF package.
JULY 5:	Mexico draws $2.5 billion from U.S. package.
AUGUST:	Mexico draws $1.73 billion from IMF package.
MID-SEPTEMBER:	The latest of loan restructuring plans, the ADE, goes into effect.
OCTOBER 5:	Mexico pays back $700 million to U.S. in 'symbolic gesture'.
OCTOBER 11:	Clinton says Mexico probably won't have to borrow any more.
OCTOBER 30:	Zedillo announces the Alliance for Economic Recuperation - labor and corporations agree to tough measures for recovery. Forecast of 3 percent growth and 20 percent inflation for 1996.
NOVEMBER:	Mexico draws $1.73 billion from IMF package.
NOVEMBER 9:	Zedillo proposes bill to set up private pension system.
LATE NOVEMBER:	Mexico launches two international bonds worth $2 billion.
1996	
JANUARY:	Mexico repays $1.3 billion to U.S.. Amount outstanding is $10.5 billion.
JANUARY 26:	Treasury Secretary Robert Rubin announces extension of U.S. aid package to August 21, 1996.

Source: *Latin Finance*, Number Seventy-Five.

deficit was unprecedented and had few parallels in recent history. Even in the aftermath of the debt crisis in Mexico in 1982, it did not cross $8 billion.

Portfolio investment inflows totalling $71.2 billion between 1990 and 1994 were used by the Mexican authorities to finance 72 percent of its current account deficit. Dependence on portfolio inflows to finance the current account deficit resulted in higher financial costs in local currency. Being a boom period, departmental stores were full of goods and consumer credit was offered on a generous scale, which increased the indebtedness of households and banks. Mexico was living beyond its means.

At this point of time two major developments (one economic and the other political) took place, which led to the collapse of the peso and later of the economy. Firstly, interest rates in the U.S. began rising in conjunction with an economic recovery which led to sudden flight of portfolio investments and short-term funds from Mexico back to U.S. financial markets. Secondly, Mexico suffered a series of political upheavals during this period which eroded investor confidence. In January 1994, there was a major armed rebellion by a peasant organisation called the Zapatistas in the southern State of Chiapas in Mexico. The Zapatistas were protesting against the NAFTA, Mexico's neo-liberal economic policies, and the lack of genuine democracy (see Box 5.3). An uncertain political environment was created as the rebels fought with the police and armed forces for two weeks before both sides agreed to a ceasefire and negotiations. In March 1994 a presidential candidate, Luis Donaldo Colosio, representing Mexico's long-time ruling party, the Institutional Revolutionary Party (PRI), was assassinated. This was followed in September 1994 by the assassination of another high-ranking PRI official, Party Secretary General Jose Francisco Ruiz Massier. In December renewed violence flared up in Chiapas. As a consequence of these political upheavals, foreign investors became cautious with their investments.

However, the emergence of the crisis had very little to do with economic fundamentals which had not shown serious deterioration in 1994. During this period Mexico's financial authorities failed to carry

Box 5.3

"Lack of Economic and Political Democracy Behind Rebellion in Chiapas"

The Indian rebellion in Chiapas is the result of three inter-related factors:

1. Economic liberalisation implemented by the Salinas Government has led to a sharp polarization of Mexican society... Economic polarisation is even more dramatic in the State of Chiapas. The Indian population in the State earns under $350 dollars per year...while its per capita income dropped 6.5 percent during the 1980s. In the nine municipalities taken by the rebels, adult illiteracy averages nearly 50 percent, while over 80 percent of the population is either homeless or lives in substandard dwellings.

2. Genuine agrarian reform never took place in Chiapas. Thirty percent of claims from landless peasants in Mexico originate in Chiapas. In December 1991 Salinas amended the Constitution, allowing communal landholdings to be subdivided and sold to private interests and corporations. Since then, big ranchers have increasingly taken over communal and Indian land with the complicity of local authorities and the use of their own private paramilitary forces. International, U.S. and Mexican human rights groups have long criticized the deployment of the army among the indigenous populations of Chiapas, where long-simmering land conflicts have been aggravated by the new agrarian policy.

3. The lack of democracy is especially pronounced in Chiapas. Indian communities are not allowed to elect their own authorities, as the vote is manipulated by the local power brokers in conjunction with the PRI. This has discredited elections as means for peaceful, democratic change...

There cannot be a military solution to the conflict. The origins are rooted in economic inequality and political authoritarianism.

Carlos Heredia

Source : Excerpted from the News Release issued by The Development GAP, 7 January, 1994.

out remedial policy measures, as Presidential elections were near, and any unpopular measure could have led to the defeat of the then ruling party's candidate, Ernesto Zedillo.

Once he was elected Zedillo's government finally moved to devalue the peso on December 20, 1994. It has been alleged that on December 18 Zedillo hinted to a few wealthy businessmen that a peso devaluation was in the offing. The next day rich Mexicans converted billions of pesos into dollars. Two days later the Mexican government announced a 13 percent peso devaluation. Coming on the heels of such a turbulent year, this move panicked foreign investors and they started pulling their money out of Mexico. Over the next two days $5 billion fled the country. The Mexican authorities failed to arrest the free fall of the peso, which plunged in value from 3.5 pesos to the dollar in early December to 7.5 pesos to the dollar by March 1995. The Mexican stock market lost one half of its value over within months of the devaluation. The crisis quickly spread to other countries in the region where stock markets also fell drastically.

Three months after Zedillo's peso devaluation, the peso had lost 50 percent of its value against the U.S. dollar. This depreciation of the peso continued despite efforts to control it by the central banks of Mexico and other countries. To deal with the situation the government issued bonds of $29 billion, called *tesobonos*.* However, these measures failed to restore the confidence of foreign investors.

The Mexican Bailout: Bailout for Whom?

Once again, Mexico approached the U.S. to bail it out from the present crisis as it had done at the time of the 1982 debt crisis. However, this time institutional investors were involved, whereas in the debt crisis foreign private banks had been involved. By the end of January 1995, with Mexico just a few days away from defaulting on its foreign debts, the U.S. arranged a $50 billion international credit. Out of this, U.S. alone promised to provide $20 billion, and the rest was to be contributed

---

* In early 1995, the Mexican government issued short-term, dollar-denominated bonds, called *tesobonos*, to raise money from investors in order to cover foreign exchange shortfall.

by the IMF, the World Bank and other G-7 countries. In return, Mexico offered its future oil export income as collateral for the borrowed funds, which were to be paid back within three to five years. Nearly $12 billion of the U.S. credit was used by the Mexican government during 1995 to retire short-term *tesobono* bonds as they matured.

Interestingly, this bailout programme came under sharp criticism from both progressive and conservative groups. Many economists, NGOs and labour groups in both Mexico and the U.S. pointed out that the bailout would award the very actors who had caused this financial crisis - the foreign investors and the Mexican government. Progressive groups, such as Equipo Pueblo in Mexico and The Development GAP in U.S., emphasised that the present crisis was not just a short-term liquidity crisis, but a bigger problem caused by the adjustment policies dictated by the World Bank and IMF. These groups argued that this was bailout of a political regime, not of the Mexican economy and its people. They strongly reiterated that:

> The current crisis in Mexico is due to the economic policies followed for the past twelve years. It makes no sense for billions of U.S. taxpayers' dollars to be thrown out into Mexico so that the old, failed and discredited policies can be pursued.[3]

On the other hand, conservatives also criticised the bailout programme initiated by the U.S. government. In the words of Lawrence Kudlow, economics editor of the conservative National Review magazine, who testified before the Senate Foreign Relations Committee:

> This is not a bailout of the Mexican peso or the Mexican economy. It is a bailout of U.S. banks, brokerage firms, pension funds and insurance companies who own short-term Mexican debt, including roughly $16 billion of dollar-denominated tesobonos and about $2.5 billion of peso-denominated treasury bills (*cites*). It is also a bailout of the Mexican government which incurred these liabilities. Finally, it could be a bailout of another $20 billion of Mexican private sector bank certificates of deposit, commercial loans and trade credits.[4]

Box 5.4

"The Mexican Model was Never Free Market"

Following are excerpts from an interview with Christopher Whalen, chief financial officer of Legal Research International (LRI), a Washington D.C. based financial services firm. The interview was conducted by Russell Mokhiber and appeared in "Multinational Monitor," April 1995.

Multinational Monitor: What lies at the root of the Mexican peso crisis?

Chris Whalen: The Mexican model was never free market. It was never designed for growth in terms of jobs or exports. It was designed solely to raise dollars, to borrow dollars. Most of these dollars were used to either pay for imported consumer products or they were siphoned offshore in the form of flight capital. [Former President] Carlos Salinas, for example, who has never held a real job in his life, leaves office with a net worth estimated in the range of several billion dollars.

MM: How did that happen?

Whalen: He has received gratuities from those below him. Carlos Hank Gonzalez, the outgoing Transportation Minister, has been in politics for 40 years. He used to own a Mexican airline. His son just bought control of Laredo National Bank. This man has billions of dollars in visible net worth - airstrips, ranches, aircraft, real estate holdings all over the world, bank accounts.

MM: Where did he get the money?

Whalen: Corruption. We believe he is one of the biggest money launderers in the country. So, you have this state that oppresses its own people, steals elections, lacks transparency, lacks a legal system that functions. And you ask yourself the basic question - why do we believe that they are going to treat foreign investors any better than they are going to treat their own people? And the answer is that there is no reason to believe that. In fact, the foreign investors once again have been badly mistreated because, by and large, of the $70 billion or so that flowed into Mexico over the last five years, perhaps as little as $10 billion or less went into real hard assets - that is, plant and equipment, capital or new factories that

contd. on next page

could produce export revenues...

MM: Where did all the money go?

Whalen: It was used to subsidise a very large current account deficit. Most of that deficit was consumer products - food, Barbie dolls - all sorts of things from offshore that they really couldn't afford. But because the Salinas government kept the peso pegged to the dollar, for a while it worked. Now, as soon as the Federal Reserve started raising interest rates last year, the game was over. The cash flow disappeared...

MM: Wasn't most of the investment from institutional investors?

Whalen: Yes, but they represent individuals. The vast majority of the $70 billion - probably $50 billion of it - was short-term portfolio investment. It was not direct investment in plants and equipment.

MM: What was the basis of your prediction two years ago that the peso would be devalued?

Whalen: Mexico was essentially a debt-driven Ponzi scheme. In other words, [Mexican government officials] were borrowing dollars, but they weren't creating any means of repayment. There were no new assets here.

The Mexican model gives free market economics a bad name. This is not free-market economics. This is corporate statism. Salinas turned public sector monopolies into private cartels run by his friends. He did not create more opportunity. He did not really open these markets to competition.

Banks in Mexico, for example, were charging people real interest rates of 30 to 40 percent over their cost of funds. What is that? That is usury. The whole system was set for a fall from the outset...

MM: Who is behind the bailout?

Whalen: Wall Street - the friends of Robert Rubin, as I like to put it. It is a subset of the group that pushed through NAFTA. It is basically Fidelity, Trust Company of the West, Alliance - they have been huge buyers of peso treasury bills. They are caught. Now, these big funds want to socialise the loss. In the past, we have been privatising the profit. I don't see them offering to give back some of their profit to help pay for this...

The Clinton administration tried to justify that the bailout programme was necessary to protect U.S. interests as well. The Treasury Secretary Robert Rubin, while strongly supporting the bailout, claimed that 7,00,000 U.S. jobs were directly dependent on the Mexican markets. Further, he argued, illegal Mexican immigration to the U.S. could increase by 30 percent, and the bailout was in the interest of "the financial prospects of all emerging markets."[5] Observers commented that Robert Rubin's foremost concern was the loss of Mexico as a model of development for other developing countries, a model which he and Goldman Sachs had advocated.[6] He told the House Banking Committee:

> Mexico has been, in several ways, a prototype for countries that are striving to put inward-looking, state-controlled models of economic development behind them... A new prosperity based on open markets, a welcome-mat for investment and privatisation is beginning to emerge... Helping Mexico through its current difficulties can keep alive the promise of market-oriented reform - the key to growth and stability over the longer term for all of us.[7]

Rubin's special interest in the bailout has also been linked to his personal background as he was co-chair of an investment bank, Goldman, Sachs and Co. before joining the Clinton administration. This bank had a major interest in Mexico as it had handled privatisation of Telephones de Mexico in 1990. It has been alleged by many commentators that Rubin personally lobbied former Mexican President Carlos Salinas to allow Goldman to handle this privatisation deal.[8]

The politics of bailout raises an important issue: Why should the governments and the people bear the costs of the crises caused by the market forces? The Mexican experience with bailout clearly shows that there was no sharing of costs by the market forces. The burden of costs has fallen on the poor citizens and the bailout has basically served only the narrow interests of elites in both Mexico and the U.S..

In fact, the bailouts set a dangerous precedence. Knowing that there are international financial institutions and governments to bail them out, the market forces continue to make risky investments which are bound to create crisis-like situations.

Impact of the Crisis

The financial crisis has led to a deterioration of the Mexican economy as well as the living conditions of the people, especially the poor. In March 1995, President Zedillo announced an austerity plan, which included imposition of higher taxes and cuts in public spending, especially in the social sectors. In addition, interest rates were raised to attract investors and strengthen the peso. As a result, interest rates peaked up at over 80 percent, which led to further decline in domestic investments by the Mexican firms. The confidence in Mexico's currency dropped so low that many domestic business houses refused to accept pesos in payment, insisting upon dollars instead.

The cumulative impacts of the austerity plan were more profound in the case of the poor people of Mexico, whose livelihoods were further threatened by job loss, fall in real wages, credit crunch, rise in prices and interest rates, and further reduction in social sector spending. In the first two months of 1995, at least 7,50,000 Mexican workers lost their jobs, and more layoffs followed in the succeeding months. The real wages of Mexican workers fell by 30 percent in 1995. According to Eugenia Corrca:

Open unemployment, which more than doubled in 1995 alone, currently stands at 6.3, as compared with 2.1 per cent in 1990. With 3 million unemployed workers in 1996, many of those who continue to be employed have had to contend with falling real wages. In this connection, real wages in manufacturing were 40 per cent lower in 1995 than in 1990. In the construction sector, employment in 1995 was 41 per cent lower, and average wages 17 per cent below their levels in 1990. The only bright spot has been on the export side, where the number of jobs has grown as a result of increased foreign direct investment and exports production. The expanding maquiladora industry currently employs more than 600,000 people in Mexico. However, the multiplier of this sector is only about two in supplier industries and local services, rather than the four or five jobs for each direct export-oriented job that is typically the case for national exporting

Box 5.5

Some Facts on the Failed Mexican Model

■ Trade liberalisation has resulted in an enormous trade deficit ($23 billion in 1993), while wiping out many domestic industries, including agricultural producers, unable to compete with the flood of cheap imports.

■ Agricultural producers have suffered from tight credit policies. Between 1980 and 1988 total credit to the countryside was reduced by one third, with the remaining credit too expensive for most small farmers to afford.

■ Privatisation and deregulation have led to a steep increase in the concentration of wealth. The richest 20 percent of the population saw their share of national income rise from 48.4 to 54.2 between 1984 and 1992, while during the same period the poorest 20 percent saw their share fall from 5 percent to 4.3 percent.

■ During the Salinas administration, the number of billionaires in Mexico rose from 2 to 24. All of them are well connected to the President, and many became super rich by taking over state-owned industries when they were privatised. The assets of the richest individual total more than the combined annual income of the poorest 17 million people. Those 17 million barely survive on less than a dollar a day.

■ Between December 1987 and May 1994 the cost of basic goods rose nearly three times as much as the minimum wage. The situation has been greatly exacerbated by the recent plunge of the Mexican peso.

■ Between 1980 and 1992, as real incomes fell, infant deaths due to malnutrition almost tripled to rates higher than those of the 1970s.

■ Until the economic crash, the World Bank, the International Monetary Fund and the U.S. Treasury hailed Mexico's adjustment program as a great success to be emulated by other Latin American countries.

Source: This information and analysis is drawn from *The Polarization of Mexican society: A Grassroots View of World Bank Economic Adjustment Policies*, a study by Equipo Pueblo, Mexico City, published by The Development GAP in December 1994.

firms in developing and industrialised countries.[9]

According to the estimates provided by the Mexican Labour Congress, the average wage has lost 54 percent of its purchasing power during December 1994-July 1995 as there has been substantial increase in the food prices as compared to other goods. For instance, before the peso crisis, the minimum wage bought 67 percent of the *canasta basic* (the basic basket of goods) for a family of five. By July 1995, it bought only 53 percent.[10]

A study conducted by *El Financier* found that in the first nine months of the Zedillo administration, 2.193 million people fell into extreme poverty. Thus, the total number of Mexicans living under poverty increased to over 40 million. Malnutrition and disease, especially among the children, has increased manifold. The percentage of children suffering from malnutrition in the age of one to four years in rural areas rose from 7.7 in 1979 to 15.1 in 1995. The deterioration in the living conditions of the poor and indigenous people has led to increased social tensions and incidents of crime.

Largely due to growing resistance by labour groups and small business houses, the Zedillo government was forced to announce some ameliorative measures. These policy measures were aimed at controlling price hike, raising wages, increasing domestic savings and public investments. In the wake of the Zapatistas rebellion, the government also announced a series of social-safety programmes which included emergency employment schemes, a credit card system and food subsidies. However, these schemes have largely remained on paper as there was no serious attempt by the Mexican authorities to implement them.

Apart from poor people, a large section of the middle class has also been affected by the growing unemployment and lower real wages. On the other hand, the rich have hardly been affected as they invested their savings in dollars. According to *Forbes,* between June 1995 and June 1996, the number of millionaires in Mexico increased by 50 percent. The wealthiest 10 percent of families, who accounted for 36 percent of disposable income in 1982 increased their share to 40 percent by 1995, according to very conservative estimates.[11]

During boom-and-bust cycles, the poor do not benefit in the boom phase as their purchasing power is almost negligible, while the rich enjoy this phase of over-consumption. The bust phase, which consists of austerity policies, brings even greater misery to the poor through job losses, fall in real wages, high inflation, high taxes and reduced public expenditures.

Even after two years of crisis, the economy was still in bad shape. Mary Purcell, an economist with Equipo Pueblo, puts it well:

> The economic data for the first three quarters of 1996 was the worst Mexico has seen in eight decades. Gross Domestic Product (GDP) fell by 7 percent. The second quarter decline was an astounding 10.8 percent. Inflation will be about 50 percent at the end of the year. On average, domestic consumption has fallen by 25 percent. Debt servicing in the first semester was an astounding $ 17.822 billion (not including payment of *tesobonos*), which is almost double what it was in the first semester of 1994. An estimated 1.5 to 2 million people have lost their jobs, and close to one-third of Mexican business has had to close its doors... Non-performing loans have increased 561 percent, as millions of businesses and consumers throughout Mexico are unable to pay their debts.[12]

Critics point out that the continuation of similar policies by the Zedillo administration has brought the economy back to the same position it was on the eve of the 1994 devaluation.[13] Even the OECD's latest survey on Mexico admits this fact. According to this survey, real GDP of Mexico did not return to its pre-devaluation level until mid-1997.

Lessons Learned

The Mexican case illustrates the dangers of over reliance on volatile, short-term capital flows to finance unsustainable current account deficits. These private capital flows are no substitute for domestic savings and, at best, can only supplement domestic resources. A country can reduce its exposure to the volatility of external capital by increasing its national savings.

Many analysts have also called for careful phasing and sequencing of import and external financial liberalisation policies. They argue that financial liberalisation policies are less likely to succeed in the absence of a sound macro-economic situation. Eugenia Correa has called for a more cautious approach to deal with the speculative capital inflows. According to Correa,

> ... far-reaching liberalisation policies are less likely to succeed if the macro economy is not soundly established. The combination of financial and import liberalisation, when undertaken in the context of loosened fiscal and monetary policies (as can happen in an election year), may lead to a boom-and-bust cycle. Such an outcome is likely to be aggravated when too much reliance is placed on speculative flows of capital to finance the boom, since such flows tend be pro-cyclical and hence flow back out of the country when conditions deteriorate and they are most needed.[14]

References

1. "Survey: Mexico," *The Economist,* October 28, 1995, pp. 4-5; Peter Passell, "Economic Scene," *New York Times,* January 12, 1995.

2. "The Boom in Portfolio Investment," *Latin American Weekly Report,* April 15, 1993.

3. The Development GAP, "Mexican Bailout a Bottomless Pit if Imposition of Failed Policies Continues," News Release, January 23, 1995.

4. Quoted in Andrew Wheat, "The Fall of the Peso and the Mexican 'Miracle,'" *Multinational Monitor,* April 1995.

5. *Ibid.*

6. *Ibid.*

7. *Ibid.*

8. *Ibid.*

9. Eugenia Correa, "Mexico's Financial Crisis and its Effects on Income Distribution and Poverty," *Globalization and Liberalization: Effects of International Economic Relations on Poverty,* UNCTAD, New York and Geneva, 1996.

10. Mary Purcell, "Mexico: One Year Later, the Crisis Continues," *Third World Resurgence,* No 67, 1996.

11. Cited in "Equipo Pueblo and the Building of Citizenship: The Mexican Crisis and

Civil Society," Mexico, September 1996, p. 6.

12. Purcell, *op. cit.*
13. The Development GAP, "Mexican Government Payback Bad News for Mexicans," News Release, January 15, 1997.
14. Correa, *op. cit.*

6

The Southeast Asian Currency Turmoil: The case of Thailand

JUST two years after Mexico faced a currency turmoil, Southeast and East Asian countries were engulfed by a similar crisis in mid-1997. The currency turmoil first started in Thailand and rapidly spilled over to other countries in the region. The Indonesian rupiah, the Malaysian ringgit, the Philippine peso and South Korean won - all came under attack. The spillover impact (also known as 'contagion effect') of the Asian currency crisis was experienced in Eastern Europe as well, where the Czech koruna was affected. The turmoil, which initially erupted as a result of the currency devaluation, soon developed into a major financial crisis in the Southeast and East Asian countries. In other countries of the region, for instance China and Vietnam, where FDI flows dominated net private capital inflows, the impact of the crisis was negligible.

Only a little while back, these countries were being touted as 'models' by the World Bank and the IMF for other low income countries to follow. In 1996, the UNCTAD too was of the opinion that the 'success'

Box 6.1

The Thai and Mexican Crises: A Comparison

In Latin America, when the Mexican crisis spread over to neighbouring countries, it was called *Tequila Effect*. When the Thai crisis spread to other countries in the region in 1997, it was called the *Tom Yum Effect* - named after the famous soup served in Thailand.

There are some similarities between the Thai and Mexican crises, but there are also many significant differences.

In both countries the underlying factors were the same - a large surge in short-term private capital inflows, rapid growth in private sector credit and growing current account deficits. Also, economic fundamentals were strong before the crisis emerged.

At the same time, there were many dissimilarities. In Thailand, the capital inflows led to increase in investments, whereas in Mexico the inflows sustained a boom in private consumption. Thus, Thailand was supplementing domestic savings with borrowings from the rest of the world to increase its productive capacity, while foreign savings flowing into Mexico acted as a substitute for her national saving. In Mexico, national saving as a ratio of the GDP came down by more than 4 percentage points between 1989 and 1994. On the other hand, in Thailand, the period 1990-95 was characterised by both higher saving and domestic investment. Various studies have found out that the deployment of capital was also much more efficient in Thailand than in Mexico.

In Thailand, the sharp devaluation and the collapse of the financial sector led to deflation in asset values, while in Mexico, although the financial sector was affected adversely by the impact of higher domestic interest rates and the devaluation of the peso, it suffered little from deflation of asset values.

Finally, GDP growth in Thailand was much more export oriented than in Mexico. Exports grew at a faster rate than the GDP in the former, but lagged considerably behind domestic production in the latter. The result was that the export-GDP ratio in Thailand showed a steady growth from 34.1 percent in 1990 to 41.5 percent in 1995. In Mexico, on the other hand, the ratio registered a continuous decline from 20.4 percent in 1989 to 16.7 percent in 1993, but showed a mild recovery at 18.9 percent in 1994.

of the East Asian countries could be replicated by other developing countries.[1]

According to Morgan Stanley Capital International, the currency crisis in the Southeast Asian countries has led to destroying of wealth worth $201 billion. It has estimated that the drop in the market values of the stocks in the Hong Kong, Korea, Indonesia and Thailand was $75, $60, $45, and $21 billion respectively between June 30, 1997 - December 31, 1997.

Various attempts have been made in the recent past to understand the causes behind the sudden collapse of the Southeast and East Asian economies. Some analysts have blamed the domestic policies of these countries, while others have questioned the role of global finance in perpetuating the crisis. However, the fact is that the crisis was the product of a combination of external and domestic factors, which globalisation aims to integrate.

Let us begin with the Thai crisis, which exemplifies for many the crisis of the export-led economic model.

The Thai Crisis: An Outcome of Weak Fundamentals?

A consensus among economists and analysts on the underlying causes of the Thai crisis is unlikely to emerge because of differing ideological perspectives, yet hardly anyone can dispute the fact that the economic fundamentals of Thailand have been performing quite well ever since it shifted from an import substituting to an export oriented strategy in the mid-1980s. In terms of all major economic indicators, except agriculture and current account and trade deficits, the Thai economy was performing well above the average during 1985-95, which is also known as the 'boom' period. As far as foreign investors were concerned, they were not disturbed by the bad performance of the agricultural sector. Their main concern was the growing trade and current account deficits of Thailand. Thailand's trade deficit as a ratio of the GDP increased from 4.96 percent in 1992 to 6.8 percent in 1995, while the current account deficit remained at 8 percent. Current account deficits become worrisome when the country is using the large inflows of foreign capital to finance domestic consumption (as in the case of Mexico in the 1990s); or just adding up the foreign exchange reserves to repay foreign debts. However, Thailand used foreign capital largely to supplement its domestic savings.

In an exhaustive review of the economic fundamentals of Thailand in the light of the currency crisis, Mihir Rakshit points out that the crisis had very little to do with the economic fundamentals of Thailand.[2] According to Rakshit, between 1985 and 1995, trends of all macro-economic and social indicators of Thailand, except trade and current account deficits, were highly positive (see Annex B). For instance:

■ With an average GDP growth of 9.8 percent per annum Thailand had the fastest growing economy in the world during 1985-95.

■ There was a gradual decline in all the indicators of external indebtedness of Thailand. The debt-service ratio, which was 31 percent in 1985, came down to 11 percent in 1995; the ratio of total debt to GDP came down from 45.1 to 42.5 percent; and the debt-export ratio from 171 to 102 percent. Thus, the argument - a country's currency could face speculative attack if it is unable to pay back its foreign debt liabilities - finds little evidence in the case of Thailand. Besides, Thailand was not placed in the category of highly or moderately indebted countries (like India or the Philippines) which could have caused a worry to foreign investors. The World Bank had put Thailand in the category of 'less indebted countries.'

■ Thailand was, perhaps, the only country in the region which had followed strict fiscal policies in the past one decade. The fiscal deficit was removed and Thailand started generating a surplus which was 2.5 percent of the GDP in 1995, quite high in comparison with 0.8 percent of Indonesia, 0.9 percent of Malaysia and (-) 0.5 percent of the Philippines.

■ The export-GDP ratio increased from 34.1 percent in 1990 to 41.5 percent in 1995.

■ A stable exchange policy was followed by the Thai authorities during 1985-95. With the baht pegged to a basket of currencies, where a large weight was attached to the U.S. dollar, this policy helped the country in two ways. First, it gave stability to the baht in comparison with other currencies, and second, it eliminated the foreign exchange risks faced by foreign investors. As a result, Thailand was able to attract a significant amount of foreign investments, especially from Japan. Besides, with the appreciation of the yen against the U.S. dollar, after the 1985 Plaza Accord,* Japanese investments in Thailand increased manyfold. This, along with the availability of cheap labour, motivated Japanese TNCs to shift their factories to Thailand.

■ The Thai authorities also maintained stability on the foreign exchange front by keeping enough forex reserves to meet at least 5.5 months' import bill during 1985-95.

■ Inflation in Thailand was very low, i.e. 5 percent. Similarly, interest payments were also very minimal.

■ Thailand also took various measures to reduce the poverty, illiteracy, infant mortality and malnutrition.

The above macro-economic indicators clearly reveal that just 18 months before the crisis the economic fundamentals of Thailand were very sound, and there was no reason to imagine that the baht would come under speculative attacks.

The Other Side of the 'Boom'

However, there was another side to the rapid economic growth under the 'boom' period. The agriculture sector had not been performing well for a number of years, and during 1994-96 its share in the GDP dropped from 4.3 percent to 3.1 percent. The poor performance of the agricultural sector led to adverse impacts on the living standards of the people staying in the countryside, as compared to their urban counterparts.

The euphoria over prosperity ran so high that serious issues such as growing regional imbalances, income inequalities and environmental degradation did not get the attention they deserved. Unlike other countries in the region, the distribution of wealth, power and opportunities in Thailand have been enormously concentrated in the capital city. Nearly 90 percent of the country's wealth is concentrated in Bangkok alone.

---

* Plaza Agreement is an agreement among the G-7 countries reached at the Plaza Hotel in New York in 1985. Under the agreement, the need to intervene in the foreign exchange markets was accepted. This agreement marks a turning point in the fortunes of the U.S. dollar as it lost its earlier gains in value against the other currencies.

Although rapid economic growth during the 'boom' period lifted many people out of poverty, poverty reduction was not equally distributed. According to estimates provided by Dr. Medhi Krongkaew of the Thammasat University, poverty became negligible in Bangkok, whereas in the Northeast region, more than 22 percent of the population lived in poverty in 1992.[3] As per these estimates, the average income of rural households in 1986 was lower than that of 1981 in absolute terms. This is the period when the rural people were worst affected, while those in the urban areas managed to make relative gains, mainly because of the export-led growth financed by foreign capital. The benefits of the 'boom' were largely enjoyed by the urban sector with very little trickle-down to the rural sector. Whatever benefits trickled down to rural areas were taken away by a small number of land owning classes. In the words of Dr. Medhi, "The boom in the property market during the last half of the 1980s also increased rural incomes, as many farmers and landowners sold their land and became relatively richer, but landless, in the short-term."[4]

Of all the income groups, only the richest gained against all others. The share of the poorest group kept falling while that of the richest group kept rising. For instance, in 1992, the share of the poorest fifth had dropped to 3.94 percent, whereas that of the richest had reached 59.04 percent. This increase in income inequalities was also contributed by the political and economic structure of Thailand. With the active support of corrupt political leaders and bureaucrats, preferential treatment, monopoly rights and favours (e.g. tax concessions) were extended to large firms as compared to medium and small firms. Similarly, development policies were distorted to favour the richer sections of society. Environmental degradation was the result of such policies.

In a significant way, the Thai 'boom' filled the unlimited desire of the elite for consumer goods. Certain industries, particularly the automobile industry, witnessed rapid expansion and Thailand began to be called "the Detroit of Asia." The country ranked third in the world in terms of sales of Mercedes-Benzes. In 1995, the ratio of Benzes to all new cars sold in Thailand was 1:9, second only to Germany.[5] Flooded with luxury consumer goods, including imported items, a chain of big shopping centres and stores was set up to cater to the affluent sections.

Stagnation in Exports

The problems with this export-led growth model began to emerge in 1996, when exports faced stagnation, while imports were burgeoning. The growth rate of Thai merchandise exports (in terms of U.S. dollar) came down sharply from 22.2 percent in 1994 and 24.7 percent in 1995 to a bare 0.1 percent in 1996, and did not display any sign of recovery in 1997. The reasons behind stagnation in the exports were many.

By and large, Thailand's exports were non-diversified, low-technology based and labour intensive, for example, clothing, leather products and agricultural produce. These exports helped Thailand to reduce unemployment, but as the labour wages tended to increase with a fall in unemployment, the exports from Thailand became uncompetitive. For instance, the minimum wages in Thailand increased by at least four to five times than those in her regional competitors like China, Indonesia and Vietnam.[6] Faced with stiff competition from these countries, which were also exporting similar kinds of goods but at cheaper prices, the Thai exports lost their competitive edge.

The problems at the export front were further compounded by a general decline in world demand in the electronics market in 1996. Similarly, agricultural exports also faced various trade barriers in the U.S., EC and other international markets. Besides, the series of floods further reduced agricultural exports as crops got damaged.

Table 6.1
International Bank Lending to Thailand*
(In billions of U.S. dollars)

	U.S. Banks	Japanese Banks	European Union Banks	Total International Lending
Thailand	5.0	37.5	19.2	70.2

* Outstanding at end-1996.
Source: Bank for International Settlements. Taken from *World Economic Outlook, Interim Assessment*, IMF, December 1997.

Another major reason for the slump in the exports of Thailand was its maintenance of a stable exchange rate pegged to a basket of currencies dominated by the dollar. As the U.S. dollar appreciated significantly against the yen, mark and other currencies, the baht also correspondingly appreciated. This overvaluation of the baht led to a severe loss of its exports to China and other countries in the region, which had devalued their currencies in the recent past.

Heavy Reliance on Short-term Borrowings

In the early 1990s, Thailand started short-term borrowings from international banks and put greater reliance on portfolio flows rather than on FDI to finance current account deficits. The short-term borrowings were largely facilitated by policy changes in 1993, when Thai companies were allowed to borrow from abroad. By August 1997 the composition of Thailand's foreign debt had become unbalanced. Out of a total foreign debt of $89 billion, $71 billion (nearly 80 percent) belonged to the private sector. With the short-term borrowings of $20 billion maturing by the end of 1997, the foreign debt was also highly unsustainable.

The burgeoning capital inflows increased the foreign liabilities of commercial banks from $5 billion to $46 billion during 1992-96, a nine-fold increase. Among the incentives encouraging borrowings from abroad were the high domestic interest rates and stable exchange rate policies. Among the lenders, Japanese banks accounted for nearly 60 percent of the total international lending by the end of 1996 (see Table 6.1).

The role of international banks in further deepening the Thai crisis needs to be looked into. According to the Bank of International Settlements, international banks ignored the warning signs of Southeast Asia's crippling financial crisis during the first half of 1997 and continued to lend money to the region. The report further informs that it was only when the major speculative attack on the Thai baht took place in May 1997 that the international commercial banks stopped lending fearing a loss. The BIS in its semi-annual report on international bank lending reported: "In spite of growing strains in Southeast Asia, overall bank lending to Asian developing countries showed no evidence of abating in the first half of 1997."[7]

Financial Fragility

The second serious structural problem of the Thai economy was the poor performance of its financial sector which absorbed a large amount of foreign capital inflows. The seeds of financial instability were planted in 1993 with the establishment of the Bangkok International Banking Facility. This facility allowed domestic and foreign banks to engage in offshore and selected onshore banking activities. With financial deregulation and greater emphasis on market forces, a major part of finance capital went to private borrowers who, in turn, extended credit to domestic borrowers. Thus between 1992 and 1996 there was a quantum jump in loans to the private sector as a ratio of the GDP, from 39 percent to 123 percent.[8] Overexposure was most marked in real estate loans, even though by 1993 the property market showed signs of overcapacity and slowdown in demand.

Taking advantage of the big differences in the interest rates between domestic and external borrowings, banks and finance companies in Thailand began taking unhedged foreign loans in foreign currencies (available at the rate of 6-8 percent) and started financing domestic companies and individuals at an interest rate of 14-20 percent in baht. Since the opportunities in productive sectors of the economy were getting reduced largely due to stagnation in exports, the banks and finance companies started financing short-term real estate businesses which witnessed a boom in the early 1990s. It has been estimated that property-related investment came to 50 percent of total investment.[9] These sources further estimate that all aspects of property development contributed between 30 and 50 percent of annual GDP growth.[10]

The movement of large private capital flows into commercial real estate was quite worrisome as earlier experiences in both developed and developing countries indicate that speculative bubbles can develop in real estate during a boom period. Asset inflation in the property sector tends to generate very high rates of return - much higher than those from manufacturing - but the returns are not sustainable in the long-run. In the case of Thailand, many manufacturers and exporters also switched

Box 6.2
Winners and Losers

Following is the list of 58 suspended financial companies. Out of these, rehabilitation plans for only two companies were approved by the Financial Restructuring Authority.

APPROVED
Bangkok Investment Plc.
Kiatnakin Finance and Securities

REJECTED
Companies suspended on June 27, 1997
Bangkok Metropolitan Trust
CL Sahaviriya Finance and Securities
CMIC Finance and Securities
Country Finance and Securities
Dynamic Eastern Finance
Finance House
Finance One
GCN Finance
General Finance and Securities
International Trust and Finance Plc.
Prime Finance and Securities
Royal International Finance and Securities
Thai Financial Trust
Thai Fuji Finance and Securities
Thana One Finance and Securities
United Finance
Companies Suspended on August 5, 1997
Asia Financial Syndicate
Bangkok Finance
Bara Finance and Securities
Cathay Finance and Securities
Cathay Trust
Chao Phraya Finance and Securities
Chatiphaibul Finance
Dhana Nakorn Finance and Securities
Ekkapat Finance and Securities

First Bangkok City Finance
Inter Credit and Trust
Krung Thai Finance and Securities
Lila Finance and Securities
Metropolis Trust and Securities
Muang Thong Trust
Multi-Credit Corporation of Thailand
Nithipat Finance
Pacific Finance and Securities
Poonpipat Finance and Securities
Premier Finance
SCF Finance and Securities
Siam City Credit Finance and Securities
Siam City Syndicate Finance and Securities
Siam Commercial Trust
SITCA Investment and Securities
Sri Dhana Finance
Teerachai Trust Corporation
Thai Finance and Securities
Thai Financial Syndicate
Thai Overseas Trust Finance and Securities
Thai Rung Reung Finance and Securities
Thai Thamrong Finance
Thai Tanakorn Finance
Thaimex Finance and Securities
Thanamass Finance
Thanapol Finance and Securities
Thanasap Finance and Securities
Thanasin Finance
Union Finance
Wall Street Finance and Securities.

their investments to real estate businesses to earn quick profits.

By the end of 1996 and in early 1997 the fall in prices of real estate (which were used as collateral for credit) had landed the majority of financial firms in serious trouble. According to the Bank of Thailand, about one-seventh of finance company lending, estimated at $6 billion, had turned non-performing by the end of 1996. However, market analysts found that the actual figure of non-performing assets was almost twice this estimate. Estimates of non-performing loans in the banking sector for 1998 run as high as 25 percent, or well over one trillion baht.[11] The Thai authorities tried to curb lending to property developers and imposed conditions for full disclosure of non-performing loans in October 1996.

In February 1997, Somprasong Land became the first company to default on a Euro-convertible debenture. This was followed by the collapse of the largest finance company in Thailand, Finance One. When it was revealed that close to two-thirds of the country's 91 finance companies were in serious trouble, the investors lost confidence, and the speculative attack on the baht was launched. Both foreign and domestic investors started buying dollars, taking advantage of the fixed exchange rate. Companies which had taken unhedged foreign loans rushed to cover their exchange risk by buying dollars forward. The Thai Central Bank sold more than $23 billions forward in a desperate attempt to defend the baht. The interest rate was also raised to discourage switching from the baht to other currencies. This move created further difficulties for finance companies.

The Thai authorities did not depreciate the baht because it was feared that this would further weaken the finance companies as their liabilities were in dollars. A devaluation of the baht would have brought more misery to these companies as they would require more baht funds to service their dollar debt. By this time, it was sure that the baht would soon be devalued.

Speculative Attacks on the Baht and Response of Thai Authorities

After periodic episodes of speculative attack in 1996, the Thai baht once again came under pressure in January-February 1997. The investors began to rethink about their investments in Thailand as they were concerned with the growing current account deficit, high short-term foreign debt, and the collapse of the financial sector. With the FIIs heavy selling in the stock markets, the share prices dropped to record low levels by 65 percent in May 1997. A situation of panic prevailed in Thai financial markets.

Anticipating a series of speculative attacks on the baht in early 1997, the Thai authorities attempted to enforce a number of capital controls. For instance, the Bank of Thailand made extensive use of the forward foreign exchange market to corner the baht available to non-resident speculators. The authorities also restricted the sale of foreign holdings of Thai stocks on the SET for baht.

Despite these measures by the Thai authorities, the strong pressure on the baht continued in May-June 1997. During this period the global financial conditions also tightened with the sudden rise in the Japanese bond yields which reduced the portfolio investments coming from Japan to Thailand.

The international financial players such as hedge funds and currency speculators are reported to have bet nearly $10 billion in shorting the baht. In a situation when large capital outflows also continued, the Thai authorities abandoned their earlier exchange rate system of pegged currency and allowed the baht to float on July 2, 1997. The floating of the baht immediately led to its depreciation by nearly 20 percent against the dollar.

In August 1997, the Thai authorities approached Japan to provide necessary financial assistance. Japanese officials declined to provide unilateral assistance but offered to participate in a macro-economic restructuring plan under the auspices of the IMF. Subsequently, the Thai government approached the IMF which approved a $17.2 billion bailout programme with stiff conditionalities. Out of this amount, the IMF and Japan were to provide $4 billion each; China, Hong Kong, Malaysia, Singapore and Australia $1 billion each; and Indonesia, Korea and Brunei another $500 million each. The World Bank and the ADB were to contribute $2.7 billion under the structural adjustment loans.[12] The full text of the letter of intent submitted by Finance Minister Tarrin

Nimmanhaeminda to the IMF is given in Annex C, while a detailed analysis of the politics of bailouts is given in chapter 8.

None of the important international financial institutions anticipated the emergence of a serious financial crisis and ignored its portents as a temporary phenomenon. In its report, *Asian Development Outlook 1997 and 1998*, which incidentally was released just before the crisis, the ADB commented:

> The slowdown in growth is in part a temporary phenomenon resulting from short-term movements in world markets and international prices which reduced trade flows between Thailand and her major trading partners. But there is also a more fundamental economic malaise caused by diminished competitiveness resulting in a loss of international markets. Even if export expansion, as forecast, revives in the near term, innovative ways are needed to improve labour force skills and to encourage the investment needed to support technology... The economy is widely perceived to be sound, and action by the authorities has probably avoided a broader monetary crisis, such as that experienced by Mexico in 1994.[13]

On the other hand, the IMF claims that it did warn Thailand as well as Malaysia and Indonesia in 1995 about the impending crisis and suggested remedial measures. According to the IMF, the Thai authorities did not follow its 'advice' of hiking the interest rates. In the prevailing circumstances, this 'advice' could have further deepened the financial crisis. This move would have led to a larger inflow of foreign funds and subsequent appreciation of the baht, thereby adding to the troubles on the export front.

Impact of the Crisis

Though it is too early to make any assessment of the cumulative impacts of the currency crisis, the available macro indicators suggest that the crisis will have a long-term impact on various sectors of the Thai economy. The IMF's conditionalities include budget expenditure cuts of about 100 billion baht; increase in the value-added tax from 7 to 10 percent;

reduction in current account deficit to 5 percent of the GDP in 1997 and 3 percent in 1998; and further reduction in subsidies and public investments. The detailed figures of budget cuts in the 1998 fiscal budget are given in Annex D.

Thailand is facing its worst recession since the mid-1980s. The country, which was used to an average growth rate of 7 percent, now faces bleak prospects of recovery. *Asiaweek* has projected the growth rate to be minus 1 percent in 1998. Domestic demand is not picking up, and there are very few buyers of consumer durables and real estate. With the devaluation of the baht, exports are likely to increase but only of those goods which have low import contents.

The Thai authorities have suspended 58 financial firms. In December 1997, the Financial Restructuring Authority announced that only 2 of the 58 suspended financial firms would be allowed to reopen and the rest 56 firms were to be closed down. (See Box 6.2). Since mid-1996, the Financial Institutions Development Fund (FIDF), a bailout arm of the Bank of Thailand, spent 1.1 trillion baht ($25 billion) to prop up troubled financial institutions. Out of this amount, baht 450 billion went to the suspended finance companies. A large portion of that amount is unlikely to be recovered. The authorities have chalked out a privatisation programme of state-owned enterprises to foot the bills of the bankrupt financial sector in consultation with the IMF and the World Bank. Under the plan, the Finance Ministry will raise money by further divesting its stakes in four blue-chip state enterprises - Thai Airways International Plc., Bangchak Petroleum Plc., Electricity Generating Plc., and PTT Exploration and Production Plc.. Besides, inflationary pressure will be there as FIDF received most of its advance money from the printing press of the central bank, by borrowings in the interbank market and from issuing short-term bonds. Eventually, taxpayers will foot the bills of the FIDF.

In the absence of new capital inflows, the domestic companies are finding it difficult to meet the liquidity crunch. Many companies have announced cost reduction measures, which largely include layoffs besides sharp cuts in wages and benefits. "We either tighten our belts or die,"[14] says Charnchai Charuvastr, the CEO of Thai telecommunications company Samart Corp., Thailand's number two paging firm. To survive, this company has prepared a plan under which the salaries of executives have been cut by 10 to 25 percent; all units have to raise cash, become self-financed and cut costs by 30 percent; or shut down.[15]

There is growing concern that the costs of the crisis are being unequally borne by the rich and poor sections of the Thai society. According to the Forum of the Poor, which is a broad coalition of people's organisations, women's groups and rural development NGOs, the devaluation of the baht, increase in the value-added tax, and the rise in the prices of public goods and services have seriously affected people in the low income groups and the poor.

Although the distribution of wealth, power and opportunities in Thailand have been enormously concentrated in Bangkok, the effects of the financial crisis are faced by villagers living far off from Bangkok - in mountains near Chiang Mai and other provinces. Farmers comprise 60 percent of the working population, but account for only 11 percent of the country's wealth. In rural areas, the small farmers have been affected by the increased cost of production because prices of agricultural inputs such as chemical fertilisers, seeds, insecticides, etc. have risen by over 30 percent, while prices of agricultural produce have not correspondingly risen.

Though Thailand's agricultural exports are expected to boom from the devalued baht, this may create further pressure on the food security of the country as it is more lucrative to grow export crops than food crops for domestic consumption. In recent years many farmers had taken loans, which were easily available before the crisis, to purchase agricultural machinery and tools. With the curtailing of spending by Thais as a result of the crisis, the prices of vegetables and other food items have sharply plummeted. Thus, these farmers are unable to repay their loans, and have landed in a debt spiral.

The worst affected by the closures and economic recession are the workers. In 1998, about 2 million people are expected to be unemployed, including at least 50,000 from the closure of finance companies. The agricultural sector is too weak to absorb laid-off workers from the cities.

The job opportunities for the poor have been further squeezed by firms subcontracting production to smaller firms and home-based workers. Workers, especially the women workers, have little choice but to accept any job, even with low wages and no benefits. Many families are finding it difficult to send children to school. The belt tightening will further lead to increase in social problems in Thailand such as prostitution. Even

---

Box 6.3

"Don't Interfere with our Economy and Politics"

Farmers are joining the growing protest movement in Thailand against the IMF-led bailout programme. Early 1997 thousands of men, women and children from the Northeast travelled to Bangkok, setting up a 'village' for three months outside Parliament House. In early 1998, the Assembly of Small-scale Northeastern Farmers, Thai Farmers Foundations Group, Assembly of Northeastern Farmers, the Alliance of Northeastern People, Northeastern Agricultural Institutions Front and the Forum of the Poor jointly issued a statement calling on the government to reveal conditions made under the bailout package with the IMF.

These six organisations are planning a protest action in Bangkok in the later half of 1998 which is expected to involve at least 50,000 people and last for a few months. The protesters plan to stay in front of Government House and Parliament and will hold a rally every evening to air their grievances.

They are demanding that the government freeze the excise tax on petrol and diesel and offset a revenue shortfall by imposing heavy taxes on inheritance and unexploited land instead. Farmers' groups in the Northeast want the government to help settle problems concerning land rights and forest destruction, debts and unfair treatment by state officials. They want fair prices for their agricultural produce, local control of natural resources, access to water and review of infrastructure projects, especially dam projects.

There is a growing consensus among these groups to oppose IMF conditionalities that interfere with and manipulate the Thai economy and politics.

child workers are affected by the crisis - many have been laid off, and others are being forced to work for less wages. In this situation the poverty in the country will increase, which will eventually lead to a widening gap between the rich and the poor.

Growing Discontent

Surprisingly, not just the ruling political party in Thailand is supporting the austerity programme, but the major oppositional political parties also do not seem to be against it. Among the trade unions, religious leaders, and some developmental NGOs as well, there seems to be an acceptance of the austerity programmes as being 'necessary.' However, there is a growing protest movement against the massive layoffs and other aspects of the austerity programme in Thailand (see Box 6.3). For instance, on January 20, 1998, some 2000 angry workers of Thai Summit Auto Parts Company clashed with the police while they were protesting against drastic reduction of their salaries and benefits. The violent nature of this protest was unprecedented in the recent history of workers' struggle.

References

1. United Nations Conference on Trade and Development, *Trade and Development Report, 1996*, United Nations, New York and Geneva, 1996.

2. Mihir Rakshit, "Learning and Unlearning from the Thai Currency Crisis," *Money & Finance*, Number 3, September 1997.

3. Medhi Krongkaew, "Income Distribution: Growth hides Rising Poverty," *Bangkok Post*, December 29, 1995.

4. *Ibid.*

5. Nuntawan Polkwamdee, "Lesson on Greed and Laxity," Economic Review Year-end 1997, *Bangkok Post*, January 15, 1998.

6. Rakshit, *op. cit.*

7. Bank of International Settlements, *Semi-Annual Report on International Bank Lending*, 1998. Quoted in *Business Standard*, January 5, 1998.

8. Rakshit, *op. cit.*

9. Rakshit, *op. cit.*

10. Ed Paisley, "Asia's Property Perils," *Institutional Investor*, January 1996, p. 61.

Quoted in Walden Bello, *Addicted to Capital: The Ten-Year High and Present-Day Withdrawal Trauma of Southeast Asia's Economies*, Focus on the Global South, Bangkok, 1997.

11. Cholada Ingsrisawang and Parista Yuthamanop, "Troubling New Era Awaits," Economic Review Year-end 1997, *Bangkok Post*, January 15, 1998.

12. Soonruth Bunyamanee and Chiratas Nivatpumin, "The Year They Sank the Baht," Economic Review Year-end 1997, *Bangkok Post*, January 15, 1998.

13. Asian Development Bank, *Asian Development Outlook 1997 and 1998*, Oxford University Press, 1997.

14. Quoted in, "Recession in Asia," *Asiaweek*, January 9, 1998, p. 41.

15. *Ibid.*

7

Contagion Effect on South Korea, Indonesia, Malaysia and Philippines

THE countries in the Southeast and East Asian region, especially Indonesia, Malaysia, Philippines, South Korea, Hong Kong and Singapore also faced currency crises following the speculative attacks on the Thai baht. The currency depreciation was much more severe in South Korea, Indonesia and Malaysia, as compared to Hong Kong and Singapore (see Table 7.1), and many governments undertook various policy measures in an attempt to stabilise their currencies. Nevertheless, the currency and stock markets in these countries continued to decline, leading to deflation and a sharp fall in the value of assets.

Let us briefly look into the nature of the crises that emerged in South Korea, Indonesia, Malaysia and the Philippines.

South Korea: Victim of Heavy Commercial Borrowings

When the Korean won faced the worst decline in recent history, it surprised many. South Korea, one of the 'miracle' stories of rapid industrialisation, was the first Asian entrant (after Japan) in the OECD-the rich man's club. The fall in the won was so dramatic that it depreciated over 50 percent between July 1997 and January 1998. Even after a $57 billion bailout programme was announced, and political support to it assured by the newly elected President in December 1997, the decline in the won and stock prices continued for several months.

The real problem confronting South Korea was not the unproductive investments in real estate and other speculative businesses, but the heavy short-term borrowings by the private sector financial institutions from foreign commercial banks. This problem got further deepened with the fall in its currency and stock prices. South Korea had relied heavily on the borrowings from foreign banks to supplement its domestic savings to meet its financing requirements.

After the mid-1990s, there has been a significant increase in short-term foreign borrowings by the South Korean banks and financial institutions. Within a short period of two and half years, the borrowings by South Korea nearly doubled, from $56 billion in December 1994 to $103 billion in June 1997. An increase of $47 billion in two and half years was very sharp indeed by international standards. European banks were the most aggressive lenders to South Korea, with their share of lending rising from 30.5 percent in mid-1996 to 35.1 percent in 1997. During the same period, the Japanese banks cut their exposure from 24.3 percent to 22.9 percent. According to the semi-annual report of the BIS, released in January 1998, almost 70 percent of bank credits granted

Table 7.1

Depreciation of Major Southeast Asian Currencies

Country	Currency	Rate/Dollar 31 Jan. '97	As on 20 Jan. '98	Depreciation in percent
Indonesia	rupiah	2375.0	10200.0	329.5
Thailand	baht	25.9	53.0	104.8
S. Korea	won	863.0	1638.0	89.9
Malaysia	ringgit	2.4	4.1	68.2
Singapore	S. dollar	1.4	1.7	24.6

to South Korea by mid-1997 were to be repaid within a year or less. Since the majority of these borrowings were short-term, nearly $70 billion were due for payments between late 1997 and mid-1998.

Faced with a situation of liquidity crunch and default, the then Korean President, Kim Young Sam, sacked his Finance Minister and replaced him with a former IMF official, Lim Chang-Yuel, on November 19, 1997. Soon after taking office, Mr. Lim announced liberal policy measures to further open financial markets and remove restrictions on portfolio investments which were introduced in the early 1990s in the wake of surge in such flows. It needs to be emphasised here that till the mid-1980s, South Korean financial markets were closed to foreign investors. It was only in 1985 that the banking sector was opened to foreign banks, and in 1987 foreign insurance companies were allowed access to the Korean markets. Later on international institutional investors and trusts were also permitted. The government allowed individual foreign securities companies to own up to 10 percent of the paid-in capital of large domestic securities companies, provided that the total stake of foreign securities companies in a domestic securities company did not exceed 40 percent. In domestic markets new financial instruments such as bonds were allowed; foreign investments in Korean stocks were only permitted in 1992 subject to strict regulations. Because of the

Table 7.2
International Bank Lending to Asia
(In million US$)

	June 97	Dec. 96	June 96	Dec. 95	Dec. 94
Asia	389,441	367,009	337,849	306,855	241,249
South Korea	103,432	99,953	88,027	77,528	56,599
Thailand	69,382	70,147	69,409	62,818	43,879
Indonesia	58,726	55,523	49,306	44,528	34,970
China	57,922	55,002	50,587	48,384	41,341
Malaysia	28,820	22,234	20,100	16,781	13,493
India	18,780	16,896	15,728	15,511	14,961
Philippines	14,115	13,289	10,795	8,327	6,830

Source: Bank for International Settlements, 1998.

inflationary pressure emerging from foreign capital flows, the South Korean authorities attempted to slow foreign portfolio investment in 1993 through the enforcement of new controls.

After announcing the removal of capital controls, the South Korean authorities had extensive discussions with IMF officials to work out a mutually acceptable bailout programme. The IMF insisted that all shaky financial institutions should be shut down as a precondition to the bailout. On the other hand, anticipating strong resistance from the labour unions to such a move and given that the elections to the post of President were due shortly, the South Korean authorities wanted to avoid an economic restructuring programme that included massive layoffs. However, a compromise was reached, and a detailed austerity programme finalised, under which Seoul agreed to slash public spending and reduce its

Table 7.3
International Bank Lending to East Asia[1]
(In billions of U.S. dollars)

	U.S. Banks	Japanese Banks	European Union Banks	Total International Lending
China	2.7	17.8	26.0	55.0
Hong Kong SAR[2]	8.7	87.5	86.2	207.2
Indonesia	5.3	22.0	21.0	55.5
Korea	9.4	24.3	33.8	100.0
Malaysia	2.3	8.2	9.2	22.2
Philippines	3.9	1.6	6.3	13.3
Singapore[2]	5.7	58.8	102.9	189.3
Taiwan Province of China	3.2	2.7	12.7	22.4
Thailand	5.0	37.5	19.2	70.2
Vietnam	0.2	0.2	1.0	1.5
East Asia Total	**46.4**	**260.6**	**318.3**	**736.6**

[1] Outstanding at end-1996.
[2] The data for Hong Kong SAR and Singapore reflect their roles as international financial centers.
Source: Bank for International Settlements. Taken from *World Economic Outlook, Interim Assessment*, IMF, December 1997.

economic growth target from 6 to 3 percent in 1998.

The South Korean case is not of the kind which the IMF usually deals with. For instance, when a country is faced with a major budget deficit, huge current account deficit and high inflation, the standard IMF conditionalities of reducing government spending, raising taxes and real interest rates may work. However, this was not the case with South Korea which had been running a budget surplus, and had a high growth rate with low inflation.

The stiff conditionalities of the IMF programme are leading to more and more bankruptcies and throwing millions of people out of work. Similarly, the IMF insistence to increase the interest rates in South Korea has led to a rise in interest rates at 19-20 percent, nearly 15 percent above the inflation rate. This move has made more companies bankrupt. A total of 17,613 companies went bankrupt in 1997. Among them are eight large *chaebol*, or conglomerates, which sought bankruptcy-court protection with combined debts of 20 trillion won ($21 billion).

In December 1997, the government suspended the operations of 14 merchant banks and an investment trust company. The large-scale bankruptcies have contributed to the rise in unemployment which increased from 2.1 percent in October 1997 to 2.6 percent in November 1997, when more than 1,00,000 people became jobless.

With the Korean domestic industry in deep trouble after the stock

---

Box 7.1

The IMF Dictionary

"IMF" has entered the Korean vernacular as a synonym for gloom, doom and despair. Some current uses:

IMF Era: Period of national humiliation

IMF Government: Hostile foreign dictatorship

IMF Sale: Deep discounts, but few buyers

IMF Syndrome: Fear of future unemployment

IMF Fashion: Used clothing

I.M.F. Fired: Black humor of the newly jobless

market crash coupled with high interest rates and deflationary pressures, many companies have very little option but to sell their stakes to foreign investors at throwaway prices and at very favourable exchange rates.

Indonesia: The Mighty Fall of Rupiah

Since the 1970s, Indonesia has followed liberal economic policies. With an open capital account, Indonesia launched major reform programmes related to trade, foreign exchange, investment and the financial sector

Box 7.2

Chronology of South Korean Crisis

JANUARY '97:	Hanbo Steel collapses under $6 bn in debts - first bankruptcy of a leading conglomerate in a decade.
MARCH:	Sammi Steel fails, provoking fears of a corporate debt crisis.
JULY:	Korea's third largest car maker Kia suffers credit crunch and asks for emergency loans.
AUGUST:	International credit ratings downgraded for banks with heavy exposure to troubled conglomerates.
OCTOBER:	Korea nationalises Kia after banks refuse to provide more loans. Standard & Poor's downgrades Korea's sovereign rating.
NOVEMBER 13:	Government denies need for IMF bailout.
NOVEMBER 17:	Won drops below 1,000 to the dollar.
NOVEMBER 19:	Seoul proposes a financial stabilisation package.
NOVEMBER 21:	Korea asks IMF for loans of $20 bn to ease debt crisis.
DECEMBER 3:	Korea signs agreement with IMF for a $57 bn bailout that includes tough conditions on economic reforms.
DECEMBER 8:	Korea's short-term foreign debt is nearly twice as big as thought, at more than won $100 bn.
DECEMBER 18:	Kim Dae-Jung, a critic of the IMF programme, is elected as Korea's President.
DECEMBER 22:	Korean state and corporate bonds reduced to junk-bond status.
DECEMBER 23:	Won falls near 2,000 to the dollar.
DECEMBER 24:	IMF and donors agree to advance $10 bn to Korea.
DECEMBER 26:	Won surges by nearly 23 percent to the dollar.
DECEMBER 30:	Foreign banks agree to roll over loans.
JANUARY 8 '98:	Further loan extension agreed.

in 1983 followed up by another series of reforms in the late '80s and early '90s. These laid more emphasis on the deregulation of interest rates, limited the power of the central bank, opened up the financial markets to the foreign banks and investors, and lifted offshore banking restrictions. As compared to other countries in the region, Indonesia deliberately kept interest rates high to attract foreign capital.

After the collapse of the baht in July 1997, it was the Indonesian rupiah that faced the worst decline as compared to other currencies. During July-December 1997, the fall in the rupiah was over 63 percent. Despite the bailout programme launched by the IMF, the rupiah continues to face speculative attacks and depreciation.

As in the South Korean case, a number of Indonesian companies had piled up substantial foreign debt before the advent of the Southeast Asian currency crisis, and a major part of this debt had a maturity of less than one year. In 1997, Indonesian companies had $55 billion outstanding

Box 7.3

Chronology of Indonesian Crisis

1997

AUGUST 14: Rupiah allowed to float. Bank of Indonesia tries mopping up liquidity with high interest rates.

SEPTEMBER 3: Rupiah under pressure and stock exchange starts to slide. Govt. freezes infrastructure projects and unveils banking reform.

OCTOBER 18: Govt. asks IMF, World Bank and ADB for advice. *"We are not asking for money,"* says President Suharto. World Bank, IMF and ADB offer $37 bn package.

NOVEMBER 1: Closure of 16 troubled banks, including one owned by Suharto's son and half-brother. Suharto's son later allowed to reopen bank under new licence.

DECEMBER 22: Moody's downgrades credit rating to junk-bond status.

1998

JANUARY 6: Rupiah collapses to 10,000 from 2,400 in August after budget breaches IMF terms. Analysts estimate foreign debt is close to $200 bn, larger than official estimate of $117 bn.

JANUARY 8: IMF announces its return to renegotiate recovery package.

in foreign debt, 59 percent of which was in the short-term category. The rupiah lost 58 percent of its value against the dollar in 1997 as Indonesian companies with heavy foreign borrowings rushed to buy the currency. With the fall of the rupiah and the increase in the domestic rate of interest to prevent capital outflows, the domestic firms that had borrowed heavily from abroad incurred heavy losses. The cost of repaying those loans has now more than doubled in rupiah terms, leaving many companies with debts they simply cannot pay.

The rupiah's slide has sent equity investors to the exit on the expectation that profits will slide. Fearing a surge in bad loans, the bank and finance stocks have fallen sharply. The Jakarta Stock Market Composite Index has sunk by 47 percent in rupiah terms in 1997, which amounts to 78 percent, if the currency's depreciation is factored in. In Indonesia, 16 banks were liquidated, and over half of 43 major · conglomerates suffered currency losses exceeding their projected 1997

Table 7.4

International Bank Lending to Indonesia
(mid-1997; $ billion)

Japan	23.15
Germany	5.61
France	4.79
U.S.	4.59
United Kingdom	4.33
Belgium	2.82
Netherlands	2.82
Austria	1.45
Canada	0.84
Spain	0.23
Italy	0.18
Finland	0.12
Luxembourg	0.07
Total	**58.73**

Source: Bank for International Settlements, 1998.

earnings.

The drop in the rupiah has further increased the total value of the foreign debt of Indonesia in rupiah terms. According to a market analyst, "It really is a vicious cycle. The rupiah drops; your foreign debt in rupiah terms rises substantially. That forces companies to reschedule debt or default, and no one wants to be exposed to that kind of environment so they start pulling their money out faster."[1]

The devaluation of the rupiah has led to sharp rise in inflation thereby increasing the living expenses of the majority of the population. In rupiah terms, the IMF-mandated elimination of state-owned monopolies, which have partially subsidised imported commodities, will lead to price jumps between 250 and 500 percent for items such as sugar, soyabeans and wheat flour. Prices of the basic food items are expected to rise in the future as the Indonesian government has accepted the IMF conditionalities to end fuel, electricity and other subsidies from April 1998. A food crisis is closing in on Indonesia. The domestic food production has been severely affected by the ongoing drought in the country. With sharp decline in the value of the rupiah, the prices of

Table 7.5
Price Shock
(in Rupiah)

Commodities	Prices as on January 15, 1998	Prices as on February 15, 1998
Rice (one kg)	1,800	3,500
Cooking oil (one litre)	2,000	5,500
Sugar (one kg)	1,600	2,200
Chicken (one kg)	4,500	6,500
Powdered milk (one kg)	6,500	19,650
Instant noodles (one package)	300	550
Bus fare (Jakarta-Surabaya)	21,000	28,000
Cough medicine (one bottle)	9,600	11,500
Soya (one kg)	1,500	3,500

Source: *Asiaweek*, March 13, 1998.

imported food items have increased manifold, leading to a triple-digit inflation. In February 1998 alone, the prices rose almost 13 percent, according to Indonesia's Central Statistics Bureau.

The shrinking economy has led to layoffs of thousands of workers in the main industrial cities of Jakarta, Bandung and Surabaya. Already nearly 15 percent of two million textile workers in Indonesia are facing layoffs as the devaluation of the rupiah has increased the cost of cotton used in the garment industry. Another cause for concern is the livelihood of thousands of construction workers who were rendered jobless as the real estate businesses went bust. It is anticipated that the unemployment figures are likely to rise to 11 percent. The prospects of unemployment coupled with rising prices has led to increasing frustration and anger among the people. " I would do anything to feed my wife and children," says Lukman, a construction worker in Jakarta faced by prospective job loss. " I want to go to war, killing those people who have caused me trouble."[2]

The workers who have been able to save their jobs are finding it extremely difficult to afford the essential items as their purchasing power has got drastically reduced due to slowdown in the economy. They cannot demand wage hikes, in the wake of price rise, as the threat of layoffs is very imminent.

Caught between prolonged drought and a raging forest fire, the poor Indonesian farmers were asked, once again, to tighten their belts under the new austerity programme as part of the IMF led bailout. Farmers in Java - where half of Indonesia's 200 million people live - have been badly affected by drought conditions. With little governmental support forthcoming, resentment among the farmers is increasing. In late 1997, a group of 50 tribal people from the remote province of Irian Jaya demonstrated in front of the Indonesian Parliament in Jakarta demanding more governmental assistance.

Once again, civil unrest is back to centre-stage in Indonesia. Fuelled by hunger and unemployment, violent food riots have become a regular feature in many parts of Indonesia. Unfortunately, the social unrest - which lacks a clear social perspective and has racial overtones - is often directed against the ethnic Chinese community, while those who have brought Indonesia to the present crisis have not been targeted so far.

Malaysia: Failed to Ward Off the Currency Crisis

Malaysia's experience with private capital flows began in the 1980s when it took steps to deregulate the economy by allowing free movement of capital. This was followed by privatisation of public sector companies and trade liberalisation.

The initial financial flows, consisting of FDI, helped Malaysia to expand its exports. Subsequently, portfolio investments also poured into the country's financial markets in the 1990s which led to appreciation of the Malaysian ringgit. In early 1994, the Malaysian authorities enforced a number of restrictions on the capital flows in order to stop appreciation of the ringgit. For instance, ceilings were put on banks' external liabilities and sales of short-term instruments to foreigners were banned. Similarly, the sale of private debt of less than one year maturity to foreigners was banned, and maintenance charges were imposed on non-interest-bearing foreign deposits. But once the speculative attempts on the ringgit were warded off, the Malaysian authorities gradually removed the controls and freed up capital

---

Box 7.4

Chronology of Malaysian Crisis

1997

MARCH 28: Central Bank restricts loans to property and stocks.

JULY 14: Central Bank stops defence of ringgit.

AUGUST 23: PM Mahathir Mohamed blames George Soros for attack on East Asian currencies: *"These countries have spent 40 years trying to build their economy and a moron like Soros comes along."*

AUGUST 27: Govt. restricts trading in the stock market. A week later, announces ringgit 60 bn fund to prop up the stock market.

SEPTEMBER 4: Govt. says several infrastructure projects will be delayed.

SEPTEMBER 5: Govt. reverses restrictions on stock market trading.

NOVEMBER 26: Ibrahim, Deputy PM and Finance Minister, unveils ringgit 500 m fund to assist troubled brokerage houses.

DECEMBER 5: Ibrahim vows to cut state spending by 18 percent; promises there will be no corporate bailouts by authorities.

flows, completely lifting all restrictions by August 1994.

As compared to earlier years, when the majority of inflows were in the form of FDI, the majority of private capital inflows to Malaysia in the mid-1990s were in the form of short-term loans and portfolio investments. Nearly 56 percent of all Malaysian loans were in the short-term category in 1997, according to the BIS. The short-term loans supplemented the domestic investments in the unproductive sectors such as consumer and property finance. The property sector loans grew faster than those in the manufacturing or other sectors. The property sector claimed the fastest loan growth at nearly 30 percent in 1996, rising from 26 percent in 1995. Meanwhile, loans to manufacturers increased only 14 percent, down from about 30 percent in 1995.

Anticipating a glut in the real estate businesses due to overcapacity and default on short-term borrowings, the speculative attacks on the ringgit began which seriously weakened it. Anticipating further weakening of the ringgit, the investors started taking out their investments from the stock markets which led to a steep fall in stock prices.

Although the Malaysian authorities intervened in exchange markets, raised interest rates, put a cap on property lending and limits on swaps by non-residents, yet these measures failed to stop the fall in the ringgit. In fact, the 'herd instinct' prevailed in the markets. Unable to stop this fall, the Malaysian government announced a series of measures to deal with the emerging crisis. Interestingly, without approaching the IMF to help it out, the Malaysian government announced an austerity programme to deal with the mounting financial crisis. This programme included:

■ Cuts in budget spending by 18 percent in 1998;

■ Postponement of big projects such as the controversial Bakun dam, the Multimedia Super Corridor, the new Kuala Lumpur International Airport, and the 2 km long 'Linear City';

■ Delay or deferment in importing luxury items, such as planes and ships;

■ Restructuring of banks, which include disclosure of non-performing assets and restraints over all credit expansion; and

■ Halting of new listings and rights issues on the Kuala Lumpur Stock Exchange.

The Philippines: Asia's Next 'Tiger'?

When the Thai property and bank sectors began to shake, tremors immediately hit Manila, where the rate of real estate development and bank lending had soared in recent years. Many investors predicted that the Philippines bubble would be the next to burst. Within days, the currency, peso, and stocks in Manila faced a sharp decline. The plummeting peso and the loss of 'confidence' among the foreign investors affected the Philippines badly. The peso fell by nearly 35 percent against the dollar during July-December 1997.

This is not the first time the Philippines is facing a sharp decline in its currency and the harsh conditionalities of the IMF. Just a decade ago, the country was in a similar situation. In 1983, the peso lost more than half its value in the span of a few months and an exodus of capital forced the country to declare a moratorium on its foreign debts. Unlike its neighbours, the Philippines has been operating under the 'rule' of the IMF since then.

The Philippines was one of the earliest East Asian countries to begin developing its financial markets, partly because of its long-standing association with the U.S.. Its money market has been active since the 1970s, its stock market was once the largest among developing countries in East Asia, and from an early date foreign banks were permitted to engage in a number of activities. The burdens of the debt crisis made further financial sector reform difficult. Net foreign capital flows from private sources essentially ceased for much of the 1980s, and the country had to rely on official assistance.

In 1994, the financial sector was further liberalised, and market-based lending was substituted for a variety of subsidised credits. Four of thirteen universal banks are now foreign owned, representing 9 percent of the banking system's assets. The abolition of all restrictions on capital repatriation and profit remittances increased investor confidence in the financial system and the economy, which in turn led to a resurgence of private capital flows.

Foreign investors returned to the Philippines, investing over $3 billion in 1993. More than half of this is portfolio investment - a higher share than in other countries in the region. The capital market has played a complementary role in privatisation: eighty-one state-owned enterprises were sold by February 1994, and many attracted foreign investors. Money is flowing in more rapidly than the economy can absorb it, as indicated by sharp increases in reserves and in the banking sector's foreign liabilities, as well as by the peso's significant appreciation in 1993 and 1994.

The weakened peso has led to increase in import costs, besides creating difficulties in the repayment of the $45 billion foreign debt. In addition, Philippine banks carry some $10 billion of dollar-denominated loans, which is about a quarter of their total loans. Should defaults arise, banks will become reluctant to lend, prolonging the credit squeeze and deepening the slump.

As in the case of Thailand (although many analysts argue that the Philippines is no Thailand), the fast growth in recent years has been in real estate businesses. The property prices have jumped 277 percent over the past five years and the potential for a property glut starting in 1998 is very much there, says a recent report prepared by Moody's Investors Services. The boom in property businesses has been largely financed by the banks. According to market estimates, nearly 30 percent of the banks' portfolios are in all aspects of property development.

Claimed to be Asia's next 'tiger' economy, growth is likely to slow down to about 3 percent in 1998 from 5.2 percent during January-September 1997. The economy may even contract for the first time since 1992, some analysts predict. The threat of recession is looming large.

References

1.   Mr. Nick Brooks, regional economist, Peregrine Securities, Singapore, quoted in "Recession holds Asian tigers at bay," *Business Line*, January 2, 1998.
2.   Quoted in "Is a Time Bomb Ticking?" *Asiaweek*, February 6, 1998, p. 24.

8

Private Profits, Public Losses: The Great Asian Bailout Programme

THAILAND was the first country in the region to approach the IMF for bailout in the wake of the currency crisis. Indonesia and South Korea followed suit soon after, while Malaysia refused to approach the IMF, largely because of Mahathir Mohamed's resistance to the IMF. The entire bailout programme, also referred to as 'The Great Asian Bailout,' consisted of over $100 billion of loans, and was unprecedented in its size. In August 1997, Thailand's package of $17.2 billion was approved by the IMF. South Korea received $57 billion, with the IMF contributing $21 billion; the Indonesian package amounted to $23 billion, of which the IMF share was $10 billion. Apart from the IMF, the World Bank, the U.S. Treasury, institutional investors and big transnational banks were involved in the preparation of the bailout programmes.

Bailouts for Whom?

As mentioned in the earlier chapter, the currency crisis, especially in

South Korea and Thailand, arose not from weak economic fundamentals, but from short-term capital flows and, therefore, the blame lies primarily with investors and commercial banks, who were funnelling in money in short-term capital and portfolio flows in these countries. When the crisis occurred they were the first ones to move out.

However, the bailout programmes were based on the wrong assumption that it was primarily the domestic borrowers who were responsible because of their heavy borrowings from abroad. The role of the lenders in the creation of this crisis was ignored. In fact, the lenders (the commercial banks) are more to blame because individual corporate borrowers cannot be expected to consider the total maturity pattern of the country's external debt in their decision making. In any international debt transaction, the lenders are supposed to analyse the commercial as well as political risks along with the maturity distribution of the country's external debt. They are supposed to properly assess transfer risks.* If they commit business mistakes, they should bear the costs like any other investor. Thus, the crisis of excessive borrowings was created as much by the creditors as by the debtors. But under the bailout programmes the discipline was imposed primarily on the debtor.

When the creditors are not made to pay the price for excessive lending, they feel encouraged to seek new avenues for similar undisciplined lending. Analysts argue that the bailout funds have further encouraged institutional speculators to continue to indulge in speculative activities contributing to the creation of an unstable international financial system, where huge funds are poured in and taken out at will. Michel Chossudovsky, Professor of Economics at the University of Ottawa, calls bailout programmes a 'social safety net' for institutional speculators. According to him, rather than 'restoring confidence,' the Thai bailout has contributed to alluring international speculators by the large amounts of fresh cash now available in the vaults of the Thai Central Bank.[1] Since August 21, 1997 a large chunk of the 17.2 billion dollars rescue money has already been ransacked and reappropriated by international

---

* Transfer risk is the danger whether a particular project will generate sufficient foreign exchange to service its foreign debts.

banks and financial institutions in a renewed upsurge of currency speculation in the course of October and November 1997.

A similar crisis is very much possible even in the U.S., where Japanese investors have put an estimated $300 billion of their savings in treasury bills and other instruments. If the Japanese investors behave in a similar way, the strong markets of the U.S. and its economy will also collapse just as those of the Southeast Asian countries did.

Unlike in the case of the debt crisis of the 1980s, the bulk of the debt was not the 'country's,' or sovereign debt, but that of the private sector companies which had borrowed heavily from international commercial banks. The crisis was not caused by government budgets but by the private markets. Even the proponents of free market ideology cannot disagree with this plain truth. But, under the bailout programme, private debt has been converted into a sovereign one, which has to be repaid by the governments and public at large. Simply put, both the private lenders and the private borrowers are being bailed out by public money. Foreign commercial banks, which would have suffered losses because of default in the repayments will not suffer any losses, thanks to bailout programmes. In fact, many lenders will be making further profits through the restructuring of banks and financial institutions taking place in these countries.

The bailout programmes in Mexico and Southeast Asian countries also highlight the fact that whenever the private sector is in trouble it expects support from the governments and public to rescue it and pay for its misdeeds. In Mexico, where the U.S. investors were largely involved and when the peso fell, U.S. investors were the first to be hit and were immediately bailed out by the U.S. government and the IMF. Thus the argument, often put forth in support of liberal and free market policies, that there should be no government interventions in the private sector's borrowings (the terms should be decided and mutually acceptable to the lender and the borrowers) holds little ground in the light of bailouts.

As mentioned earlier, these governments were following liberal policies in relation to foreign borrowings. The crisis could have been avoided had the South Korean or Thai governments intervened and put curbs on the private sector's short-term external borrowings. But then the Bretton Woods institutions would have disapproved such interventions by the governments. Now, these same institutions are seeking intervention by the governments of these countries to bail out the lenders as their money is at stake. Again, this is against the rules of the free market which says that those who have made mistakes should pay for them. At the same time, when it comes to supporting ailing domestic banks and financial institutions, these institutions insist that the governments play by strict market rules. Thus, under the bailout programmes, the foreign banks alone are given huge subsidies so that they do not have to suffer for their mistakes, while local banks and companies are forced to go under. Furthermore, the bailout programmes encourage commercial banks to continue risky lending as they know that the IMF and national governments are ever there to bail them out if a crisis occurs.

One would have expected the governments of Southeast Asian countries to have simply washed their hands off the problem by arguing that the matter was between the private borrowers and lenders, and they could not be involved in rolling over or repaying private foreign debt. But the governments of these countries lack the political will to take such a stance, and instead voluntarily approached the IMF for bailout funds.

Role of the IMF

The role of the IMF in the Asian bailout programmes has come under sharp criticism. Not just progressive and left circles, surprisingly, even staunch upholders of free market and globalisation policies are critical of its policies. Some of these criticisms, which are very valid, are given below:

Wrong Medicine, Wrong Treatment

Firstly, the underlying principle behind the IMF led bailout programmes does not suit the current crisis. The IMF is providing bailout funds with conditionalities to impose fiscal discipline. Thailand, Indonesia and South Korea had already devalued their currencies before the bailout programme and therefore this was not demanded by the IMF. Other conditionalities, such as raising of interest rates, tightening of credit and cuts in public spending were included. These conditionalities could be effective in countries which have higher budget deficits or large public debts. In the case of the Southeast Asian economies, the standard IMF medicine will not work because the nature of crisis is different. In these countries, the problems lie not with the fiscal indiscipline of the government (in fact, many of these countries have experienced fiscal surpluses), but with the individual companies of the private sector. With the imposition of severe fiscal discipline, the deflationary pressures on the economy are likely to increase. Similarly, the IMF condition to increase the interest rate to lure foreign investors will prove to be counterproductive, as many companies will simply go bankrupt, which will make it more difficult for the corporate sector to recover.

Thus, any programme of recovery will depend on the recovery of the private sector which can be managed if the confidence of investors and depositors is restored and currency rates are made stable. A cut in public spending will lead to further slow-down of the economies and widening inequalities. The IMF programme insists that South Korea slow down its rate of growth to 3 percent per annum and have a fiscal deficit of no more than 1 percent of GDP. In the case of Thailand, the IMF has laid down the condition that it is to produce a cash surplus equivalent to one percent of its GDP in the year 1997-98. The prospects of economic growth in these countries in the near future are doubtful. In addition, the link of growth with equity, which these countries have been able to establish in the past, are getting broken under the IMF programme, as job losses and the incidence of poverty increase manifold.

Table 8.1
The Costs of Bailouts *(in $ billion)*

Country	Cost	Contributions		
		IMF	U.S.	Japan
South Korea	60	21	5	10
Indonesia	23	10	3	5
Thailand	17.2	4	-	4
Philippines	1	0.7	na	na

IMF Conditionalities Carry WTO Agenda

The IMF bailout packages for Indonesia, Thailand and South Korea carry conditionalities that are linked to the agenda of the World Trade Organisation. These programmes include components such as market access and trade-related measures which are part of the negotiations at the WTO.

In the case of South Korea, the IMF's keenness to ensure that WTO agreements are complied with is clearly evident in its agreement of 5 December 1997. The conditions imposed by the IMF include specific measures under the WTO to liberalise trade. The bailout programme clearly states: "Timetables will be set, in compliance with WTO commitments, at the time of the first review, to eliminate trade-related subsidies; eliminate restrictive import licensing; eliminate the import diversification programme; and streamline and improve the transparency of the import certification procedures." The Korean authorities have already taken steps to abolish the type approval test system for imported vehicles thereby opening its local markets to foreign car makers. In the Indonesian bailout programme, a key element is the "liberalisation of foreign trade and investment." The medium-term programme for further reduction of tariff barriers includes those on a number of items previously excluded. In its eagerness to get the bailout funds, the Indonesian government promised the IMF that over the next three years all remaining non-tariff barriers, other than those necessary for security, safety and health reasons, will be phased out. Similarly, the insistence that Thailand and South Korea increase foreign ownership in the financial markets lies outside the framework of IMF macro-economic conditionalities. South Korea , which had restricted foreign ownership in its domestic financial markets as well as imports of goods from Japan, will now have no choice but to open up its financial markets and allow import of goods from Japan.

With the implementation of these conditionalities, the financial companies, especially from the U.S., will be the biggest gainers as the U.S. has been putting pressure on South Korea to open up its financial sector for a long time. The U.S. and Japanese contributions in the Korean bailout programme gives them enough leverage to open up its markets. The role of U.S. and Japan in taking undue advantage of the crisis in South Korea has been criticised by the media there.

What the U.S., Japan and other developed countries were unable to attain, for many years, through bilateral negotiations or under the WTO, they have very quickly achieved through the IMF programme within a few short weeks. As Professor James Tobin of Yale University and winner of the Nobel Prize for economics, puts it,

> It is hard to escape the conclusion that the countries' currency distress is serving as an opportunity for an unrelated agenda - such as the obtaining of trade concessions for U.S. corporations and expansion of foreign investment possibilities.[2]

IMF's Dual Standards

The IMF is criticised for adopting dual standards while dealing with the lenders and debtors. The IMF programmes insist that these countries cannot provide any financial support to their ailing banks and financial companies but should allow them to go bankrupt. However, when it comes to foreign commercial banks and financial institutions which have lent the money, the IMF does not insist that the same principles be followed. On the contrary, it would like the countries to repay all the loans with interest to the lenders. That is why analysts have called the IMF as "the chief debt collector for international banks."[3]

Furthermore, analysts have pointed out that the IMF took just two weeks to chalk out a $57 billion package for South Korea, while it took years to get an agreement on less than $10 billion worth of debt relief to poor countries falling under the category of Highly Indebted Poor Countries.

IMF: Part of the Solution or Problem?

Despite the massive bailout programme worked out by the IMF and followed by the recipient countries, the economies of these countries are not recovering. On the contrary, the currencies and stocks continue to plunge. Thus, the premises on which the bailout programmes are designed have come under sharp criticism. Economists like Jeffrey

Sachs have demanded greater transparency from the IMF to explain its methodology for working out the bailouts, while the Prime Minister of Thailand has called for a review of the IMF plan. "The premise on which the terms (of bailout programme) were based have changed. And we will ask if the IMF has a plan to review it," said Chuan. The IMF medicine is not working in Thailand and Indonesia where investors are losing confidence and currencies and stock markets have become further unstable.

The IMF's complete control over economic decision-making and management in these countries became evident when Indonesia announced its plan to introduce the currency board system in order to halt the fall of the rupiah. The IMF, supported by U.S. and other G-7 countries, put tremendous pressure on the government to defer this plan. It even threatened to suspend the entire bailout package if Indonesia went ahead with the proposal. The currency board system represented a direct challenge to the institutional dominance of the IMF as this system would have made it totally irrelevant.

Growing Criticism of IMF

Unable to bring economic recovery in the region, the IMF has become the target of criticism even from true believers in free market and globalisation policies. For instance, Harvard Professor Jeffrey Sachs, who has spent his professional life in advocating 'free market' and 'shock therapy' economic reform measures, recently said that when an economy is in crisis, "the first thing to remember is not to call the IMF."[4] He argued that the Fund's deflationary, tight-money policy prescription handed down to these governments is not the correct solution to the problem. Financier George Soros, by no means ideologically opposed to the IMF prescription, criticised the IMF for its role in the bailout programmes in the Asian region. According to Soros, the private sector is ill-suited to allocate international credit, therefore, a new institution, International Credit Insurance Corporation, should be set up which will guarantee international loans up to a point deemed safe by it.

Even the World Bank, the Fund's twin sister, criticised the IMF for its bailout programme. The World Bank's chief economist, Mr. Joseph

Stiglitz, publicly criticised the IMF (which is extremely rare) for imposing bailout programmes consisting of higher interest rates, less government spending and higher taxes. He warned that such measures could "push these countries into severe recession." On the eve of its President, Mr. James Wolfensohn's tour to six Asian countries in January 1998, the World Bank statement said that the absence of effective social safety nets threatens efforts to lift millions of people out of poverty and risks sending millions of others into the poverty endured by previous generations. Public spending is the only way to ensure adequate social protection, it said.

Similar views were also expressed by the political leaders of Thailand and Malaysia during the ASEAN Summit in Malaysia in December 1997. These leaders were of the opinion that bailout programmes have not yielded the expected economic recovery, on the contrary, they have worsened the situation leading to growing public resistance against IMF programmes in the region, especially in South Korea and Indonesia.

In the U.S. too, the IMF and the Clinton administration have been criticised for the bailout programmes. Apart from criticisms by NGOs, labour groups and women's groups, the bailouts have also been severely criticised by the Democrats. "We cannot support a bailout that imposes

---

Box 8.1

"The IMF is a UFO"

About 30 percent of the Thai children believe that the IMF is an unidentified flying object (UFO). According to a survey of 1,648 children under the age of 15, conducted by Bangkok's Rafabhat Institute Suan Dusit, only a quarter of all children surveyed actually knew what the IMF was. Children in Thailand are mystified by the IMF.

The survey showed that the children are facing the impact of the economic crisis. Some 55 percent said their parents were giving them fewer toys, and their families were dining out less. 26 percent of children surveyed said their fathers had become more short-tempered, and 32 percent said their mothers were stricter than they used to be. A further 21 percent said they were getting less pocket money.

an economic stranglehold on working people, tramples democratic rights, ignores the underlying causes of instability, and then asks the American taxpayer to foot the bill,"[5] said David Bonior, a Democrat in the U.S. House of Representatives. The Republicans have also criticised the IMF and the Clinton administration for the bailout and accused the policies of the IMF and the Clinton administration as being "part of the problem, not the solution" in Asia.

Therefore, there is a widespread feeling in the region and elsewhere that rather than policing global finance capital on behalf of the people, the IMF is policing the people on behalf of global finance capital.

Role of the U.S. in Bailout Programmes

The U.S., which has played an important role in the success of Southeast Asian economies through market access, security support and economic aid in the past four decades, however, was reluctant to intervene in the bailout process. Given the fact that the U.S. has a dominant position in the IMF's policies (the U.S. controls nearly 28 percent of IMF's total capital), it along with Japan pushed the IMF centre-stage and made only a small contribution in the bailout fund. When the demand for an Asian Fund was suggested by many ASEAN countries in the wake of the crisis, it was turned down by the U.S. on the grounds that the IMF has enough resources and expertise to handle such crises. It seems that the U.S. strategy was to remain invisible in the Asian crisis while pushing its own agenda through the visible IMF. In a behind the curtain role the U.S. administration monitored the developments in the region. According to the *New York Times*, the discussions to deal with the Asian crisis involved not only bankers, fund managers and trade policy analysts , but also foreign policy-makers, security and strategic policy analysts and intelligence chiefs.

In the case of South Korea, the U.S. role was more visible in pushing ahead its own agenda for removing restrictions on foreign investments in Korea's financial markets in the bailout programme, a fact acknowledged by the Korean authorities. In December 1997, when the bailout plan was yet to be worked out, the South Korean Finance Minister admitted: "We must recognise the reality that a plan which the

U.S. does not support will face difficulty passing the IMF board, even if the IMF working level team and the Managing Director agree." When an IMF team arrived in Seoul in November 1997 to negotiate the terms of a bailout for South Korea, a senior official from the U.S. Treasury also checked into the same hotel. IMF staffers kept in touch with the Treasury official as they hammered out the deal with the Korean government. The final package represented a joint Fund-Treasury policy framework.

Similarly, in the case of the Indonesian bailout, the U.S. pushed its demands which were later included in the overall programme. However, Thailand was peeved with the U.S. for not contributing financial resources to its bailout programme, whereas Indonesia and South Korea had received U.S. support. The statement by the U.S. that it played a key role in the preparation of the Thai plan at the IMF was not taken seriously by Thai authorities. "At the moment, the U.S. has done nothing to help Thailand, to be very direct," chief government spokesman of Thailand, Akapol Sorasuchart, is reported to have said. The Thai authorities were expecting the U.S. to participate in the bailout programme as Thailand has been one of the region's closest U.S. partners. Thailand was the first country in Asia to establish diplomatic relations with the U.S. in 1833. Besides, Thailand has a special treaty with the U.S., the 'treaty of amity' since the Second World War and which has been amended and updated from time to time. This treaty gives American citizens and investments a national treatment allowing them special privileges to operate in many areas of business, apart from the financial sector and that pertaining to national security.

In a voice of bitterness, Dr. Panitchpakdi, Thailand's Deputy Prime Minister on a recent visit to India, recounted how the U.S., whom Thailand regarded as a trusted friend, let it down in a moment of crisis:

> ... we had this treaty with the U.S.... This treaty of amity gives everything away, you see. This treaty is something special that Thailand has given to the U.S... When they took away our GSP, I asked for some special treatment, but they said 'no.' I asked, "How about the treaty of amity." They (still) said "no special

treatment." It is not special treatment, it is something they should give us back (in return for the continuance of the treaty)... In the former Government, when I was the Deputy Prime Minister, I proposed the amendment of the treaty of amity... The U.S. administration was very agitated. They said, if Thailand amended the treaty, then other countries... would also revoke this treaty.[6]

Given the harsh conditionalities linked with the total bailout programme, the Thai authorities are finding it hard to meet the IMF condition that the country achieve a budget surplus equivalent to 1 percent of its gross domestic product in the fiscal year 1997-98. The country has already slashed its planned budget for the year to 800 billion baht ($16.63 billion) from 982 billion baht, but government revenues have fallen quicker than expected as the economy plunges into recession. As a result, the Thai authorities asked for renegotiations of the terms of the bailout which was rejected by the U.S. administration and the IMF. This has further led to tension between the U.S. and Thailand.

In many ways, the Asian currency crisis has contributed in the strengthening of the U.S. dollar in the world currency markets. The crisis has brought back the almighty dollar as everyone wishes to have dollars in the Asian region. In Asian countries with current account deficits and high debt levels, the demand for dollars has substantially increased. Corporates are buying dollars to meet future debt repayments as there is a fear that the dollar will be more expensive later on. Given the fact that much of Asia's debt is short-term, it has to be paid or rolled over soon, which means the region needs a large and continuing supply of dollars.

On the supply side, however, only few international investors are at present willing to invest or sell dollars into Asia, while local companies are not bringing their money back to the region. Exporters will either use their dollars to fund their own debts or hold them offshore in expectation of their local currency falling more, in order to earn more profits. The mad rush to buy dollars can be seen even in Singapore, which has current account surpluses and large foreign exchange reserves. People in Singapore are switching their savings accounts into dollars. With the Asian markets in turmoil, Europe in an economic funk, and the price of just about everything falling around the world, it seems everyone wants to have and hold dollars.

Role of Institutional Investors, Speculators and International Banks

Along with the IMF, the international institutional investors and international commercial banks, which should be held accountable for contributing in the creation of the currency crisis in the region, were actively involved in the designing of bailout programmes. Since these institutions had a vested stake in averting the loan default by the domestic financial institutions in Southeast Asia, they were regularly consulted by the IMF, the World Bank and the U.S. Treasury while designing the bailout programmes.

The demands of these institutions to further deregulate Korea's financial markets and open up bond markets to foreign capital were incorporated in the macro-economic package of the bailout programme. For instance, the proposal to repackage as government bonds much of short-term debt that South Korean banks owe foreign lenders was proposed by J.P. Morgan & Co.. A rough draft of the J.P. Morgan plan was presented to bankers in New York and to the Korean government on the next day. J.P. Morgan's aggressive advocacy for such a proposal was criticised by many bankers and market observers. Said one banker also involved in the talks: "When this thing first broke, Morgan seems to have already decided what they wanted to do next... That sort of surprised me, because it didn't seem to me that was where we were. I think for a bunch of bankers to sit around New York and decide what the Koreans need without talking to the Koreans is a little nutsville."[7]

Similarly, the idea of guaranteeing the debts of commercial banks was also proposed by J.P. Morgan & Co.. Since these proposals of international banks received political backing from the U.S. government and Bretton Woods institutions, the Korean authorities agreed to offer government guarantees on the private debt and provided incentives such as higher interest rates in order to transfer the short-term debt with foreign banks to medium and long-term debt. In an interview with a newspaper, Finance Minister Lim Change-Yeul was quoted as saying,

"We need to provide incentives such as higher interest rates in order to transfer the short-term debt with foreign banks to medium-term and long-term debt. We also plan to offer government guarantees on the debt as requested by the foreign institutions as a condition to converting the debt."

When U.S. President Bill Clinton convened a meeting in December 1997 to discuss whether the U.S. should 'bail' out South Korea, these institutions played a key role in the formulation of the U.S. position. A U.S. official has been quoted as saying: "You could tell this was New Age foreign policy because the assessment didn't come from the CIA. It came from J.P. Morgan." According to media reports, the Federal Reserve Bank of New York had extensive consultations with the officials of U.S. commercial banks including Chase, Bank America, Citicorp and J. P. Morgan, while European and Japanese banks had closed-door meetings to evolve a common position to deal with the situation.

George Soros (he often describes himself as a 'stateless statesman') played an important role in putting pressure on the Korean authorities when the Korean President, Kim Dae-Jung invited him to 'advise.' After meeting the President, Soros showed his interest in investing nearly $1 billion if a total restructuring of the Korean economy took place with emphasis on opening up of the economy to foreign investors, changing labour laws and further deregulating the economy.

Who Benefits from Bailout Programmes?

Although Asia's economic crisis is perhaps the worst global financial shock since the 1930s, yet it is seen as a great investment opportunity by the international commercial banks, TNCs and financial institutions. According to a survey conducted by Price Waterhouse, nearly 51 percent of 377 chief executives of TNCs, contacted in November and December 1997, identified Asia as a region in the world offering the greatest business opportunities. In the words of Robert Hormat, vice chairman of Goldman Sachs International, "Thanks in part to the Asian crisis, we are in the midst of the most competitive environment in world history."

When the crisis occurred, some TNCs operating in the region suffered short-term losses as many of their projects were shelved (for instance, ABB lost the controversial Bakun dam project in Malaysia). But, in the long run, TNCs have emerged as the net gainers because labour costs and assets in dollar terms have sharply declined in the wake of currency depreciation in these countries. "Our bottom line is hardly affected at all," says Maurice R. Greenberg, Chairman of AIG, an insurance TNC. He views Asia's turbulence as an opportunity to acquire stocks, bonds, and if possible, entire companies in the region. The decline in the labour costs (in dollar terms) benefits foreign companies to shift their production base to the region, while the decline in assets and market value of domestic companies enables foreign investors to buy these companies for a song. Rather then starting a new company buying the existing companies at cheaper rates makes economic sense because one can get all the distribution, market, brand-name recognition and trained labour force free. On the other hand, the international commercial banks have been assured that they will get their money back with better returns and government guarantees.

To facilitate foreign ownership and takeover of domestic companies in these countries, the IMF has imposed conditions which ask for greater accessibility and ownership rights to foreign companies. For instance, Thailand was asked to allow foreign banks to own more equity in the local banking sector. In October 1997, the Thai government announced it would allow foreign institutions to hold a majority stake in local financial institutions. Thailand is now permitting 100 percent ownership besides privatising state enterprises. Recently, the Bank of Thailand announced that foreign investors taking a majority shareholding in local financial institutions will gain equal rights as Thai firms in property ownership as well. The IMF agreement with Korea consists of conditions which make for foreign takeover of its companies. The agreement calls for removing the curbs on the ceiling on individual foreign ownership to 50 percent by the end of 1997, and to 55 percent by February 1998. The Korean authorities have opened the bond market to foreigners. At present, a three-year corporate bond is being traded at 20 percent of the annual interest rate, which is a good return despite the downside risk associated with foreign exchange. The bulk of the money will go for repayment of the short-term debt of private sector borrowers to foreign lenders. This scenario is well explained by Michel Chossudovsky:

> As the scenario is developing, foreign commercial banks will not only not suffer any losses from their imprudent lending, but are salivating at the prospects of earning fees on the inevitable restructuring of the Korean private sector. In a way, the IMF conditionalities themselves call for this. The government has already agreed to give total freedom to foreign capital to buy equity in the corporate and financial sectors in Korea. Vultures would be gathering to pick up corporate entities at throwaway prices.[8]

The Great Asian Sale

A number of banks, buildings, blue-chip and bankrupt companies are on sale at heavy bargain prices in the region. Prices are down up to 60 percent from pre-devaluation days. Assets which were earlier barred to foreigners, such as banks and real estate are on sale. In fact, there seems to be a mad rush by the foreign investors to buy the domestic companies in these countries. Interestingly, buyers are not all western companies. A number of Asian companies, including a few state-owned enterprises, are also looking for acquisitions in the region.

■ AIG, the U.S. insurance giant, has bought Bangkok Investment, one of the two survivors of the mass closure of 56 companies. The other suspended companies will be sold soon.

■ Singapore's state-owned enterprise, DBS, took over Thai Danu Bank. The DBS bought 60 percent of equity in Manila's Bank of Southeast Asia in January 1998 for $40 million. Singapore's two other government-linked corporations, Singapore Telecom and Singapore Power, are looking for acquisitions in the region.

■ The Coca-Cola company has picked up 5 percent more of its Thai bottling operations, raising its stake to 49 percent and 100 percent of its bottler in Korea.

■ Korea has launched privatisation of Steelmaker POSCO, Korea Telecom, Korea Heavy Industries and Construction, Korea Gas and others. The U.S. financier George Soros, who is also an 'informal adviser' to President Kim Dae-Jung, has shown interest in buying public corporations of Korea that have been privatised.

■ GM and Daewoo, once opponents, have signed an exclusive agreement to discuss a new joint venture.

■ Societe Generale Asset Management of France bought an 85 percent stake in Japan's Yamaichi International Capital Management.

■ Pepsico has shown interest in taking over Haitai Beverage Co. Ltd., an affiliate of Korea's insolvent Haitai group.

■ The mega-merger between Thailand's two cable TV operators - International Broadcasting Company and UTV Cable Network Plc.- has led to a virtual monopoly power over paid television in the country.

■ The Hanwha Group of Korea is selling its oil refineries to Royal Dutch/Shell after having sold half its chemical joint venture to BASF of

---

Box 8.2

Growing Suicide Fever in South Korea

In a Confucian society that equates failure with dishonour, at least one South Korean businessman is committing suicide every day, according to the Korean Federation of Small Business, a lobby group for small and medium size industries in South Korea. The number of business related suicides is expected to be 400 in 1997 as bankruptcies increase in a foundering economy. The federation said 13,500 small businesses were declared bankrupt in the first ten months of 1997.

The IMF bailout programme, with its stiff conditionalities, is expected to lead to further bankruptcies next year, with up to a million or more people thrown out of work. "The life of small business owners has always been harsh, but the IMF will make their life miserable. The number of suicides may increase further because of worsening economic conditions dictated by the IMF," said an official of the federation.

Small businesses have always had trouble obtaining finance from South Korean banks, because nearly two thirds of the banks' available money is sucked by major conglomerates. In recent weeks, a lot of financially troubled banks have tightened their credit policies, making it even harder for small businesses to obtain loans.

Germany.

- Procter and Gamble Co. recently obtained a controlling share of Ssangyong Paper Co., in what is believed to be the first large takeover of a South Korean company by a foreign firm.

- Robert Bosch, a German industrial company, has bought control of its joint venture with the Kia motor group.

- Thai Petrochemical is looking to sell its cement plants as it struggles to meet debts. Foreign companies such as Westdeutsche Landesbank, of Germany, and Credit Suisse-First Boston, the firms bidding for Finance One, are putting forward their offers for the shares of Thailand's shattered financial market.

- On 26 November 1997, the American financial institution, Citibank signed a memorandum of understanding with First Bangkok City Bank and said it planned to buy a stake of at least 50.1 percent.

- Taiwan's Core Pacific bought the healthy Hong Kong operations of Japan's failed Yamaichi Securities.

Who Loses?

The public at large is suffering under the impact of the bailout programmes as public spending has been slashed and taxes have been increased. Among the major sufferers, the workers are the worst affected. The conditions stipulated in the programmes include the cutting of jobs in order to provide more freedom to companies. As per the programme, financial institutions in the region are being closed down or suspended (56 finance companies were closed in Thailand, 16 banks were closed in Indonesia, and 14 merchant banks were suspended in South Korea), leading to the loss of thousands of jobs. Countries such as Thailand, Indonesia and South Korea have also launched massive privatisation programmes to meet the IMF conditions under the bailout programme. In order to invite foreign capital to buy these public sector units, the governments have to first shed 'excess' workforce. These factors have significantly contributed to the depression of wages and the weakening of the bargaining power of labour unions. With the economy already in recession, and a freeze on domestic credit, many sectors of the economy are facing stagnation and new job opportunities are now very meagre.

According to the I.L.O., unemployment is going to surge in Asia in the coming years: several million people are going to lose their jobs in Thailand, South Korea and Indonesia, while nearly one million Filipino workers will be forced to return home from neighbouring countries when work is not available. And those who manage to hold on to their jobs will see real wages drop significantly became of inflation, says the organisation.[9]

With decline in the standard of living, massive unemployment and real decline in wages, social conflict in these countries is sharpening. In the case of South Korea - where the workers have been in the forefront of the pro-democracy movement and have earned labour rights after years of struggles - they have protested against the massive layoff schemes offered by the IMF. But even they have now consented to labour reform measures permitting retrenchments under certain conditions. Unlike South Korea, labour unions in Thailand and Indonesia have little public support and are not well organised. It is unlikely that the labour reforms in the name of 'labour market flexibility' will be opposed in Indonesia and Thailand.

Closing the Door to Foreign Workers

During the boom periods, many Southeast Asian governments welcomed cheap workforce from neighbouring countries. The rapid economic growth was, to a large extent, made possible by the migrant workers. For instance, Malaysia had nearly 2 million foreign workers (8,00,000 of them illegal) mainly from Indonesia, Philippines and Bangladesh. With the financial crisis looming large over these economies, the governments have started deporting a large number of foreign workers to make space for the locals in the job market. In Malaysia, no new work permits have been issued for skilled workers since August 1997. In January 1998, the Thai Prime Minister approved a proposal to expel the country's 9,86,000 illegal workers, most of them from Myanmar, by 1999. Besides, the number of registered foreign workers will also be reduced. Similarly, South Korean officials have already shipped out 50,000 foreign workers and are planning to deport another 1,00,000 more in the coming months.

These measures only help the ruling elite to divide the workforce on ethnic lines and divert their attention from the structural weaknesses of these economies.

References

1. Michel Chossudovsky, "The IMF's 'Social Safety Net' for the Institutional Speculator," *Third World Resurgence*, No. 86, 1997.

2. Quoted in N.C. Menon, "Vulture Capitalism," *The Hindustan Times*, January 12, 1998.

3. See, for instance, Martin Khor, "IMF: Bailing out Countries or Foreign Banks?," *Third World Economics*, Issue No. 176, 1-15 January 1998.

4. Quoted in an editorial,"IMF - at the Receiving End," *The Hindu Business Line*, January 13, 1998.

5. Quoted in "A Top Democrat Threatens to Fight IMF's Bailouts," *International Herald Tribune*, January 16, 1998.

6. Excerpted from his speech given at The Partnership Summit in Chennai, India, on January 9, 1998. Also appeared in, "Supachai: Thailand's Voice of Bitterness," *The Hindu Business Line*, January 14, 1998.

7. Quoted in, "Bankers Seeking Profits May Increase South Korea's Options," *Wall Street Journal*, published in *The Financial Express*, New Delhi, January 5, 1998.

8. Michel Chossudovsky, "The IMF Korea Bailout," (via e-mail), December 1997.

9. Neil Behrmann, "Unemployment Bogey Looms in Asia: ILO," *The Hindu Business Line*, 2 March, 1988.

9

Will India go the Southeast Asian Way?

WILL India go the Southeast Asian way? This question is being hotly debated among the policy-makers, financial institutions, NGOs and economists in India. The immediate response of the government was to state that chances of a currency turmoil in India were very remote because of the strong differences between the Southeast Asian economies and India. The very first statement of Dr. Bimal Jalan* after taking over as the RBI Governor was, "we will not go the Southeast Asian way as the economic fundamentals of the country are strong." As elucidated earlier, the Mexican and Southeast Asian crises have very little to do with the economic base or the economic fundamentals of these countries. These crises are the outcome of the unfettered

---

* Dr. Bimal Jalan was, till recently, India's Executive Director at the World Bank. When the United Front government came into power in 1996, he joined the Planning Commission as its member. In December 1997, he was appointed as the Governor of the RBI by the United Front government headed by I.K. Gujral.

mobility of short-term capital flows.

However, as India has recently attempted to integrate its financial markets with the rest of the world, its chances of getting affected by the developments in the rest of the world have increased considerably. To illustrate: when the stock market witnessed the worst ever crash on 19 October 1987 India was not affected by it as our financial markets were not open. But when the stock prices crashed on 27 October 1997, stock prices crashed in all Indian markets as well. This crash in the Indian markets was the result of global integration, and cannot be attributed to sudden changes in the economic base. Two lessons emerge from the global integration of Indian markets: what happens all over the world affects the Indian markets; and when markets crash world-wide panic takes over and fundamentals are ignored. It is in this context that the impact of the Southeast Asian crisis on the Indian markets has to be seen.

Moreover, the financial liberalisation of Indian markets with heavy reliance on hot money flows will have serious implications for the financing of current account deficit, a fact to which the policy-makers cannot remain blind. Although the current account deficit in India is now less than 1.5 percent of GDP, as compared to Thailand's 8 percent, this low figure is bound to increase when the domestic industry comes out of the recession, and the quantitative restrictions on consumer good imports are removed under pressure from the WTO.

Many experts feel that the slower deregulation of the financial sector in India has proved to be the saving factor and has protected the economy from getting engulfed by the Asian turmoil. As India opens its door for hot money flows, it will become more susceptible to the currency crisis. Given the fact that about 85 percent of forex reserves in India are accounted for by hot money flows, the country cannot afford to be complacent about removing controls and restrictions on inflows.

Spillover Impact of Southeast Asian Currency Crisis on Indian Rupee

Fears of a fresh fall in the rupee's exchange rate vis-a-vis the U.S. dollar surfaced immediately after the Thai devaluation. A strong lobby, largely consisting of exporters and corporate houses, demanded depreciation of the rupee. It was argued that this would boost India's exports which have become uncompetitive due to the devaluation of the currencies of many Southeast Asian countries and that of the Pakistani rupee.

However, the plain fact is ignored that despite heavy devaluation of the Indian rupee by 115 percent during 1990-97, the exports have not picked up. Moreover, the process of competitive devaluation can go on endlessly as Pakistan, or any other neighbouring country, can keep devaluing its currency to remain competitive. In the case of the Thai currency, when it appeared weak, the speculators further drove it down. As a result, FIIs started pulling out of markets, new flows stopped and the spillover impact led to a crisis in neighbouring Southeast Asian countries.

The cumulative result of fears and rumours was the sharp fall of the rupee from Rs. 36 to the dollar in November 1997 to Rs. 39 to the dollar in early December 1997. According to the RBI, the dramatic fall in the rupee was due to intense speculation by banks and corporates in the forex market. The RBI has found that the speculators were arbitrating between the call and foreign exchange markets, which was creating an unnatural demand for the dollar in the forex market and putting pressure on the rupee. But putting all blame on the speculators for the fall of the rupee is not correct. In fact, the RBI supported the depreciation and viewed it as a "mere correction of the cumulative real appreciation of the rupee." However, in an attempt to prevent further fall of the rupee below Rs. 40 a dollar, the RBI aggressively intervened in the market, but in this process lost $2.66 billion of foreign currency assets.

The depreciation of the rupee has come under sharp criticism from many analysts who argue that this will not help exports in the long run but will only increase India's foreign debt by Rs. 4,00,000 million. Besides, it will contribute to a hike in oil and fertiliser prices thereby increasing inflation.[1]

The impact of devaluation will be very severe in the case of power projects of independent power producers (IPPs). The devaluation will lead to an increase in IPP tariffs as the project cost will increase on account of foreign currency denominated financing, capital equipment and imported fuel. Thus, the State Electricity Boards (SEBs) will have to buy power at higher IPP tariffs. Given the bad financial health of the SEBs, the increase is likely to be passed on to the consumers.

India's Recent Experiences with Hot Money Flows

With the introduction of liberalisation policies in 1991, India has witnessed a significant surge in private capital flows. Prior to 1991, capital flows consisted largely of foreign direct investments, official aid flows, commercial borrowings and Non-Resident Indian (NRI) deposits. FDI was limited, averaging around $200 million a year during 1985-91, and restricted to certain sectors of the economy. Since capital markets were closed to foreign investors and the only entry available was through listed country funds, a limited amount of foreign portfolio investments were routed through a small number of offshore funds. For instance, the Unit Trust of India floated the first offshore fund, called the India Fund in 1986, which was listed in the London Stock Exchange. Subsequently, many asset management companies floated offshore funds to invest in India. These funds were largely registered in tax havens, such as Cayman Islands and Mauritius, to avoid the taxes on dividend and capital gains.

With the government's policy shift from official borrowings to foreign investments (as it does not entail a debt service burden), measures were taken up to attract foreign investments in the form of both FDI and portfolio investments. In February 1992, the government announced that Indian firms can also raise funds through equity and convertible bond issues in Euromarkets. In September 1992, the government allowed portfolio investments in the Indian capital markets by permitting Foreign Institutional Investors (FIIs) to access capital markets on registration with the Securities and Exchange Board of India (SEBI). Till January 1998, 481 FIIs were registered with the SEBI.

Portfolio Investment overtakes FDI

The liberalised policy measures towards foreign investments have mainly led to a surge in portfolio investments in India. Although during the post-liberalisation period FDI flows have also increased, the growth in portfolio investments has been more dramatic (see Table 9.1). In not a single year since 1992-93 have the FDI flows outnumbered the portfolio investments. In 1993-94 and 1994-95, the portfolio inflows were many times more than the FDI, contributing over 70 percent of the total capital inflows during this period. Private capital inflows currently comprise 19.1 percent from ECBs and GDRs, 28.4 percent from FDIs, and 52.5 percent from FIIs and NRIs.

Compared to Latin American and East Asian countries, the capital inflows into India have two distinctive features. First, contrary to its East Asian neighbours, where a large share of the inflows consisted of foreign direct investments, inflows into India are mostly portfolio investments. Second, unlike Latin American countries, where short-term capital and bank deposits dominate, inflows into India consist of investment in equity and debentures, which are costlier to reverse, both because of the differential taxation on short- and long-term capital gains and because significant sudden market reversals could imply capital losses. A large number of investments by FIIs have been routed through Mauritius, which provides tax concessions as India and Mauritius have

Table 9.1

FDI and PI in India *(in $ million)*

	1991-92	1993-94	1994-95	1995-96	1996-97[P]
Foreign Direct Investment	150	620	1314	2163	2609
Portfolio Investment	8	3493	3581	2214	2775
F. I. I.	0	1665	1503	2009	1855
Euroissues/GDR	0	1463	1839	149	900
Others [a]	8	365	239	56	20
Total Direct and Portfolio Investment	**158**	**4113**	**4895**	**4377**	**5384**

P: Provisional.
a. Includes NRI portfolio investments, offshore funds, and others.
Sources: Reserve Bank of India; Ministry of Finance, *Economic Survey*, 1996-97.

signed a double taxation treaty.

Surge in External Commercial Borrowings

The external commercial borrowings (ECBs) are also on the rise as Indian corporate houses prefer raising cheap foreign loans. This list includes big Indian companies such as Reliance Industries and Birla AT&T Communications. Since the foreign borrowings come cheaper, many companies have used ECBs to retire their high cost rupee debt. This works out to be much cheaper given the wide gap between the domestic and overseas interest rates. However, due to the recent depreciation of the Indian rupee in December 1997, many companies such as SAIL, Bombay Dyeing, IPCL and MSEB have deferred their plans to seek ECBs, while a number of other companies, such as BPL Telecom, Flex Industries, ITC and Gujarat Ambuja, are going ahead with their plans to borrow from abroad.

However, despite the surge in portfolio investments in India, the investor base has remained very narrow. The bulk of funding has come from regional and country funds aimed primarily at individual equity

Table 9.2
The Top Ten Euroentrants

Company	Offer Date	Offer Size *(in $ million)*	Offer Price *(in $)*
VSNL	March '97	500	13.90
SAIL	March '96	370	13.00
SBI	Oct. '96	370	14.20
Reliance Industries	Feb. '94	300	23.50
ICICI	Aug. '96	230	11.50
Larsen & Toubro	Nov. '94	150	15.40
Reliance Industries	May '92	150	16.40
BSES	Feb. '96	136	14.40
Larsen & Toubro	Feb. '96	135	16.70
Indian Rayon	Jan. '94	125	15.40

Source: *Business Today*, December 22, 1997-January 6, 1998.

investors. During 1993-94, 11 India-dedicated country funds were launched, raising a total of $2.7 billion. These funds were targeted mainly at individual investors in the U. S. and U. K.. Portfolio investments from Japan have been limited in part because Indian stock exchanges have not yet been approved by the Japanese Ministry of Finance, while most Asian investments have originated from Hong Kong. Analysts have found that very little interest has been shown by pension funds and other institutional investors.

As the government has not been able to aggressively push the privatisation programme in India, largely due to labour pressure, equity flows have largely remained in the private sector. Although FIIs have purchased equity in a few public sector companies (e.g. VSNL and SBI), which have issued GDRs (see Table 9.2), the service as well as manufacturing sectors have received the majority of portfolio investments.

Hot Money Flows Constitute 80 percent of Forex Reserves

Over the years, the proportion of hot money flows to forex reserves of India is steadily increasing. It increased from 37.50 percent in 1994 to 53.52 percent by March 1997, and then further to 78.80 percent by February 1998.

The stock of potentially hot money can be arrived at by adding the stock of short-term debt, investments by FIIs, issuance of GDRs, and offshore funds. According to the RBI annual report for 1996-97, India's short-term debt was $6.7 billion (as per the BIS estimates, India's short-term debt was $7.75 billion at the end of June 1997). Similarly, the GDR figure as on March 1997 was $5.4 billion and the portfolio investments amounted to $8.8 billion. These figures add up to a staggering $20.9 billion, against forex reserves of $24.1 billion. In other words, the hot money flows constitute a whopping 86.7 percent of India's total forex reserves. This figure is very high as compared to a maximum of 60 percent recommended by the CAC committee. Undoubtedly, this figure has further increased in recent months as a result of the interest rate surcharge on credit for import finance. Besides, there are non-bank short-term liabilities. Many analysts have estimated that the ratio could well be close to 100 percent. "If we take all the latest figures into account, chances are that the ratio may even exceed 100 percent," said S.S. Tarapore, head of the CAC committee.

Similarly, there has also been a deterioration in the adequacy of reserves in terms of import cover. In March 1991 forex reserves were barely adequate to meet 2.7 months of imports and this figure improved to 8.6 by 1994. Then it again declined to 6.9 months by March 1997.

By and large, Indian policy-makers have not taken serious note of this phenomenon as they think that there is no need to panic. Given the

---

Box 9.1

Forex Reserves: Adequate Enough?

The CAC committee had suggested four parameters to judge the adequacy of foreign exchange reserves in India.

1. Reserves should not be less than six months of imports;

2. Reserves should not be less than three months of imports plus 50 percent of annual debt service payments plus one month's import and export;

3. The net foreign exchange assets (NFA) to currency ratio should be not less than 70 percent; and

4. The short-term debt and portfolio stock should not exceed 60 percent of reserves.

Forex Reserves as on February 13, 1998=$24.1 billion

Adequacy Measure	Actual	Norm (CAC Committee)
Reserves to average monthly imports (imports of latest 12 months)	7.2 months	6 months or more
3 months of imports+50% of annual debt service payment+1 month of import and export	$24.1bn	$22.8bn or more
Short term debt and portfolio stocks to reserves (%)	86.7	60 or less
NFA to currency (%)	73	70 or more

Source: *Business Standard*, February 26, 1998.

fact that India's short-term debt is increasing and there is always the danger that investors may begin to withdraw at the slightest hint of a speculative attack, the policy-makers should not be complacent and off guard.

Growing Dominance of FIIs in Indian Markets

Increasingly, the domestic institutional investors are voicing their demand for a level playing field between them and the FIIs. Although there are over 480 FIIs registered with the SEBI to operate in Indian markets, only a handful of FIIs dominate the markets. As the cumulative portfolio investment in India by the FIIs till November 1997 was about $9 billion, just five top FIIs contributed over 40 percent of the total investments (see Table 9.3). These five FIIs are Morgan Stanley, Capital International, Jardine Fleming, Schroders and Templeton. Recently, the $259 billion (assets managed) Capital Group has overtaken Morgan Stanley in India as the largest FII in India, riding on a spate of high-velocity investments in a host of Indian stocks, most of them in the past few months.

According to *The Economic Times,* Capital International has $1.8 billion worth of total India exposure, while Morgan Stanley currently stands at $1.5 billion, excluding its India domestic fund worth roughly $177 million. Capital is the largest FII in Reliance Industries (holding 3 percent of the equity capital), as well as in Hindustan Lever and MTNL, where the investment would be more than 5 percent of the equity capital. Capital set the courses ablaze some time ago when it bought

Table 9.3
Top FIIs in India

FIIs	Investment *(in $ billion)*
Capital International	1.8
Morgan Stanley	1.5
Jardine Fleming.	0.8
Schroders	0.6
Templeton	0.5

Source: *The Economic Times*, December 8, 1997.

close to Rs. 400 crore worth of RIL shares in a single week. Morgan holds dominant positions in companies such as HDFC (once close to 10 percent) and Shriram Honda. Jardine Fleming, Schroders and Templeton, the other three FIIs, have dedicated country funds with Jardine as the leader.

In recent years, many FIIs have also carried out mergers and amalgamations with domestic institutional investors, which has further helped the FIIs to consolidate their strength in the Indian markets. The recent mega-mergers include Morgan Stanley with India's top domestic investment company, JM Financial; Merill Lynch with DSP; Goldman Sachs with Kotak Mahindra; and Lazard with Credit Capital. The merger of JM Financial - which has a strong presence in the Indian markets - with Morgan Stanley has surprised many market analysts. In its attempt to find reasons behind this merger, a recent editorial in *Business Standard* says,

> Nimesh Kampani is an influential and well-connected figure on the Indian financial scene. His company, JM Financial, tops the domestic league table for investment banking. As a mobiliser of funds it ranks second after SBI Capital Markets. And it is close to the top in other rankings as well. If it still feels the need for a tie-up with a foreign investment bank and brokerage firm, it is because of the changing nature of the Indian market. Corporates needing money would like to look at both domestic funds as well as the international market. And the broking business will have to depend on business from foreign institutional investors as well as local players. When customers operate across national boundaries because capital markets are getting integrated, the intermediaries in those markets must be equally integrated...[2]

Wider Implications

The inflow of foreign portfolio investments through Foreign Institutional Investors (FIIs) and Euroissues have had a strong impact on the Indian securities market. In fact, in the last few years (1992-95), FIIs have influenced market movements to the maximum extent. Although India has been able to attract not more than 5 percent of the total capital flows to emerging markets, as the bulk has gone to Latin America and Southeast and East Asia, yet the impacts of these flows on the Indian financial markets have been very profound in many ways.

The entry of FIIs has weakened the strength of domestic institutional investors in India. On the one hand, the entry of FIIs has led to the growing role of institutions in Indian markets which historically have, by and large, remained retail and individual based. On the other hand, with huge amounts of financial resources at their disposal the FIIs are the

---

Box 9.2

UBS largest FII in Indian Debt Market

The Union Bank of Switzerland (UBS) has emerged as the largest FII in the Indian debt market with a net investment of Rs. 229.55 crore. UBS has a 100 percent debt fund approved for investments up to $350 million (Rs. 1375 crore). Compared to the total approval given to the fund, UBS' net investments are low. The fund made purchases of Rs. 616.21 crore, and divested Rs. 339.31 crore, bringing its net investments to Rs. 229.55 crore.

The other top FIIs in debt markets are HSBC Asset Management Hong Kong Ltd. and Peregrine Capital Ltd.

The total funds approved by the SEBI amount to $2018 million (Rs. 7890 crore). But the net consoli-

dated investments at the end of 1997 were Rs. 449.31 crore. The total purchases by all the funds at the end of the year were Rs. 1,089.59 crore with sales of Rs. 640.28 crore.

The SEBI has given final approval to 10 funds and in-principal approval to 5 funds. These include J. Henry Schroeder Bank ($150 million or Rs. 589 crore); Morgan Grenfell Trust Corporation ($200 million or Rs. 785 crore); Templeton Investment Counsel Inc. ($90 million or Rs. 353.25 crore), Credit Suisse-First Boston (Cyprus) Ltd. ($200 million or Rs. 785 crore), Alliance Capital ($200 million), and Chescor International ($50 million).

real prime movers in the Indian stock markets. Except a handful of major public sector financial institutions, such as UTI, no Indian institutional investor can match the resources of the FIIs. With retail business almost vanished, any action by the FIIs (whether buying or selling) determines the movements in the markets nowadays. Moreover, the recession has also badly affected the financial markets, leaving very little business with the domestic players. Squeezed between the falling retail demand and the FIIs' growing dominance in the markets, the Indian brokers in the capital markets are moving to other businesses. For instance, 27 brokers resigned from their proprietary status between April 1996 and March 1997 at the Bombay Stock Exchange. These brokers, who used to be the rulers of the Indian stock markets, are shifting to businesses such as animal husbandry and garment manufacturing. A recent newspaper article described brokers as "Broken Masters of the Universe." Says Naresh Aggarwala, who was till recently the largest domestic institutional broker in North India,

> I am pulling out of the business. I may be giving up my membership cards at all the exchanges soon... I recommend to all my fellow brokers that until there is a level playing field for the domestic broker, don't waste your money here... Profits and losses, we can take in our stride. The real issue is the coming in of the FIIs who call themselves investors... I have suspended my activities until such time as the regulators give up their fixation for foreign companies..

With the policy-makers still relying on the investments by FIIs, it is ignored that these investments are not reliable and sustainable. For instance, when India depreciated its currency in the wake of the Southeast Asian currency crisis in November 1997, the FIIs were the first to react to these developments and started selling stocks. According to the SEBI, for the first time since India opened its doors to FIIs in 1992, net FII investments in India have turned negative in November 1997 - that is, there was an outflow of FII funds. As a result, the cumulative FII investments into the country dipped to $8.96 billion in December from $9.13 billion in November 1997. In the entire month of November '97, the FIIs were the net sellers.

Sensing a longer period of political instability in India, many FIIs have already pulled down their shops and are moving out of the country, and those who wanted to come on board are rethinking their strategies. This has negatively affected the overall investment environment in the capital markets besides creating joblessness among the professionals,

---

Box 9.3

When 'Blue-eyed Boys' went Jobless

Name: Rajat Gupta. Age: mid-twenties. Qualification: MBA from a reputed institution. Address: A posh locality in Bombay - Cuffe Parade or Malabar Hills. Car: Opel Astra. Monthly salary: Rs. two lakhs. Job: Investment banking, equity and finance.

Rajat Gupta was one of the many professionals hired by the FIIs to do equity research, project appraisal and forecasting. He was having a nice time. However, in November 1997, his boss flew down from Hong Kong to tell him - and others - to pack up. Rajat's story is not uncommon and the list is growing. After suffering losses in the Southeast Asian stock and currency crisis, the FIIs do not wish to take any risks in India, which has recently witnessed political instability and depreciation of the rupee. Besides, the depressed stock markets and year-end redemption

pressure are the other reasons for the FIIs to leave the country.

Daewoo Securities has stopped its operations in India; Peregrine India retrenched 100 employees; DMG India, the investment banking arm of Deutsche Bank, put down its shutter, and WI Carry cut its staff by 10 percent. Besides, the world-wide mergers and acquisitions among investment firms have further created the reasons for downsizing in the Indian operations. Following the mergers of their parent companies, BZW and Natwest Markets, as well as the Union Bank of Switzerland and SBC, the employees of these companies are now facing an uncertain future.

With no alternative job prospects immediately available, it has been a traumatic experience for the 'blue-eyed boys' of the Indian financial markets.

Box 9.4

FIIs and GDRs: Nothing 'Unethical' About it !

FIIs have been accused of following unethical practices by the Indian companies which recently issued GDRs in overseas markets. The VSNL, which recently issued GDRs, has put a formal complaint to the SEBI to take action against the five FIIs - Morgan Stanley, Fledgling Nominees, Robert Fleming, ILF Mauritius and Jaguar Funds, which according to the VSNL, offloaded a sizeable amount of their holdings before the launch of its GDR and thus brought its price down, and consequently the price of the GDR.

As VSNL was planning a GDR issue worth U.S. $500-600 million towards the end of 1996, and the timings of GDRs cannot be kept secret, the FIIs started selling the script, which consequently dragged the GDR price down. The VSNL's share price fell by 30 percent, from Rs. 1,327.50 on 22 July, 1996 to Rs. 940 on 18 October, 1997.

Given the fact that the FIIs are in an advantageous position, as they can sell in the Indian markets (thus bringing down the price of the share), and buy the same shares in the international markets at much cheaper rates, the FIIs were doing the same with the VSNL GDR issue. Such 'unethical' practices are part of sound business strategy of the FIIs.

STEP 1

FII buys Indian company's shares at Rs. 220 per share. FII interest takes the share price up, to Rs. 250.

STEP 2

Enthused company decides to try Euroissue at 80 percent of the Indian market price on the day the issue opens. 80 percent of Rs. 250 = Rs. 200.

STEP 3

Getting news of coming Euroissue, FII sells heavily, at an average price of Rs. 230, but creating a bear run that drives price down to Rs. 200.

STEP 4

Euroissue price falls to 80 percent of Rs. 200=Rs. 160. FII uses the proceeds of its sale at Rs. 230 per share to pick up the same company's Euroissue shares at Rs. 160.

STEP 5

Net result : FII makes Rs. 10 profit per share (he bought at Rs. 220 and sold at Rs. 230), plus gets the shares back Rs. 70 cheaper in Europe. And the Indian company can raise far less money than it had hoped for from its Euroissue.

Courtesy: Shekhar Ghosh, "Hooked, Lined and Sunk," *Outlook*, November 6, 1996.

who were the 'blue-eyed boys' of the corporate world. (See Box 9.3).

Furthermore, analysts have also found that the volatility of stock prices has increased with the entry of FIIs in the capital markets. According to a recent IMF cross-country study of emerging markets, stock price volatility in India has increased since FIIs have been permitted to participate.[4] This study compared the period 1976-May 1992 with the period 1992-February 1994, when the FIIs were permitted to invest.

Apart from gaining control over the Indian capital markets, the FIIs are also accused of manipulating the GDR issues of Indian companies. The FIIs have been accused of unethical manipulations by VSNL which recently issued GDRs. Given the global mobility of funds at their disposal, the FIIs were dragging the domestic price of the scrip down, and consequently the GDR price down, and moving the money generated from the sale of the scrip out to Europe to pick up the shares of the same company cheaper in the Euroissue. (See Box 9.4).

Capital Controls in India: Towards Deregulation

Given the volatile nature of portfolio investments, the Indian government introduced a number of regulations and controls in 1992. As part of its 'prudent external debt management,' the government discouraged short-term commercial loans from abroad. However, simultaneously the government announced a series of policy measures, which largely included giving more space to FIIs to operate in the Indian markets, as well as removing restrictions on the external commercial borrowings by the companies.

Till 1996, some of the regulations guiding the FIIs in India included: FIIs must register with the SEBI and RBI; FIIs are not allowed to invest in unlisted securities and government securities; FIIs are not permitted access to the forward foreign exchange market; total FII investment should not exceed 24 percent of any company; an individual FII is not permitted to invest more than 5 percent in a company; capital gains taxes* - 10 per cent on long-term capital gain (over one year) and 30 per

---

* A tax paid on the increase in value of an asset between its purchase and sale.

cent on short-term capital gain - were introduced for FIIs. Similarly, the government had earlier announced special regulations for Indian companies keen to access the Euromarket for equity funds and commercial borrowings through the issue of Global Depository Receipts and other instruments.

However, the government has gradually removed many of these regulations, especially during 1996-97. The Finance Ministry in June 1996 announced fresh guidelines which allow Indian corporates, especially those in the key infrastructure sectors, far greater flexibility in accessing commercial debt and equity funds from abroad. All infrastructure projects will be permitted to access ECBs up to 35 per cent of their total project cost. In the case of power and other infrastructure projects, even greater flexibility has been introduced. For instance, the new guidelines have allowed infrastructure projects in oil exploration and telecommunication sectors greater flexibility in accessing ECBs of a minimum five-year average maturity. This is a shift from the earlier policy which allowed corporates to access ECBs of not less than an average seven-year

Box 9.5

The Securities and Exchange Board of India

The multi-million stock scam in 1992 as well as the growth of stock markets in India have led to the establishment of a separate regulating agency, the Securities and Exchange Board of India. The SEBI was largely formed on the pattern of the Securities Exchange Commission of the U.S. to protect the interests of investors in securities and to promote the development of and to regulate the securities market. The functions of the SEBI include registering and regulating the working of stock brokers, sub-brokers, share transfer agents, bankers to an issue, trustees of trust deeds, registrar to an issue, merchant bankers, underwriters, portfolio managers, investment advisers and mutual funds. The other functions of the SEBI include prohibiting insider trading in securities, and regulating substantial acquisition of shares and takeovers of companies. The FIIs are also registered and regulated by the SEBI.

maturity. Besides, companies involved in these projects can use their foreign borrowings to fund their project-related rupee expenditure.

Similarly, the government has further reduced the maturity period for 100 percent export-oriented units which can now access ECBs at an average three-year maturity as compared to a seven-year maturity earlier. The ECB limit for exporters has been further increased from $15 million to $100 million. Thus, the old policy of 'prudent external debt management' has been replaced by the new policy of global integration through deregulated capital inflows.

Moreover, the Indian authorities have recently announced plans to introduce new financial instruments such as derivatives in the Indian markets. In this regard, a committee headed by Mr. L.C. Gupta was set up to introduce derivatives trading in India. However, many analysts

---

Box 9.6

The Deregulation of Capital Flows in 1997

Following is the list of the major policy measures taken by the United Front government to deregulate and liberalise the private capital flows in 1997.

- Individual limits for FII investment in a company raised from 5 to 10 percent;

- The definition of FII widened to allow proprietary funds and endowments;

- FIIs allowed to invest in unlisted companies and government securities;

- FII debt funds permitted and forward cover allowed;

- New ECB window for up to $3 million opened for corporates without end-use restrictions;

- The ECB limit for exporters increased from $15 million to $100 million;

- Higher ECB limits for infrastructure projects including for rupee expenditure, introduced;

- ECBs of more than 10-year maturity period kept outside; cap on overseas borrowals; and

- SEBI-registered mutual funds allowed to invest in overseas markets.

have warned that in the absence of an effective and consistent regulatory framework for the derivatives markets, the financial system may fall prey to speculators. Such concerns have also been expressed by the Mr. M.G. Damani, President of the Bombay Stock Exchange and a member of the L.C. Gupta committee. In a dissent note Mr. Damani warns against a premature introduction of derivatives trading in India which will result in massive drainage of foreign exchange from the country. Between the hedging demand of foreign institutional investors and the interest of the nation, the latter is more important, he says.

Dangers of Capital Account Convertibility

The government's keenness to introduce full Capital Account Convertibility (CAC) in India will have serious implications on the outflows of hot money. In February 1997, the government appointed a committee headed by S. S. Tarapore to examine the issues related to CAC. In its report submitted to the government in June 1997 the committee has called for full CAC by the year 1999-2000, provided that a few preconditions, like a lowering of the fiscal deficit, a low inflation rate, adequate level of 'owned' forex reserves, and reduction in non-performing assets of the banking sector etc., are met. (See Box 9.7).

Since the committee's recommendations are in tune with the ongoing policy of financial liberalisation, it has received tremendous support from the FIIs, banks, trading and business houses and international financial institutions. With the government showing its eagerness to implement the recommendations of the committee, the preconditions suggested by it are unlikely to be met in the face of the lack of political will and instability. The Southeast Asian crisis should serve as a lesson to policy-makers to rethink about the introduction of full CAC in India.

Most analysts agree that the Thai and South Korean crises were also contributed by failing banks and non-banking financial institutions. Fortunately for India, banks are, till date, not allowed to invest significantly in real estate business. However, the net non-performing assets (NPA) of the Indian banks are quite high, around 17 percent. If one compares the net NPAs with the net worth of banks, the picture is gloomy. For the State Bank of India net NPAs, as on 31 March 1997, amounted to 56.7

Box 9.7

What is Capital Account Convertibility?

In simplest terms, Capital Account Convertibility means free inflow and outflow of capital. CAC refers to "the freedom to convert local financial assets into foreign financial assets and vice versa at market determined rates of exchange." CAC already exists for non-residents and foreign investors in India. As per the Tarapore committee, CAC will have a different meaning for different entities - for individuals, corporates, banks, investors, etc.

FOR INDIVIDUALS

- Anyone can borrow from NRIs and open accounts abroad.
- Any individual investor can subscribe to foreign currency deposits.
- NRIs can repatriate their non-repatriable assets.

FOR CORPORATES

- Companies can issue additional equity overseas without seeking prior permission from the RBI.
- They can also issue dollar bonds or deposits.
- They can invest in bonds of any currency.
- Takeovers of companies in foreign countries with investment upto $50 million allowed.

FOR BANKS

- Access to foreign currency loans up to one-year maturity made easier.
- Banks can fund businesses overseas at their discretion.
- Banks can accept deposits in foreign currency.

FOR INVESTORS

- Investment institutions can expand their horizon to even the New York Stock Exchange with overall ceiling going up to $2 billion.
- FIIs now need not seek FERA approval from the RBI every 5 years.
- No more maturity restrictions for FII investment in debt.

FOR FINANCIAL MARKETS

- Forex markets get a major boost with an expanded business.
- Dealing no longer exclusive preserve of banks.
- Derivatives allowed.
- Government securities market becomes liberalised.

Source: Compiled by the author through various reports and documents including *The Report of the Committee on Capital Account Convertibility*, June 1997 and *The Economic Times*, June 4, 1997.

percent of its net worth. For Canara Bank, the figure was 65.5 percent, for the Bank of Baroda it was 74.4 percent; for Punjab National Bank it was 107 percent; and for Dena Bank it was 78.3 percent.[5] A significant portion of their net worth will vanish if banks are forced to write off their NPAs.

The other problem related to Indian banking is the relatively low level of provisions against NPAs. For instance, the provisions, as a percentage of total assets, amounted to only 1.04 percent for the public sector banks in India, as compared to Korea's 1.5, Malaysia's 1.2 and Thailand's 0.22.[6] If the downtrend in the Indian economy persists, the NPAs will erode the capital base of the banks.

To avoid a Southeast Asian like crisis from emerging in India, the government will have to take measures to reduce the NPAs. Similarly, efforts will have to be taken up to restrict the free movement of short-term funds in response to interest rate differentials. Otherwise, massive capital inflows would encourage lending for speculative purposes, with disastrous results as happened in Thailand. Thus, the crisis of Southeast Asian countries emphasises the need for more regulation on the use of funds by the banking sector for real estate and other speculative purposes.

However, instead of learning lessons from the Mexican and the Southeast Asian crises, and consequently adopting policy measures to avert a similar crisis in the country, the Indian government is going ahead with its plan of financial liberalisation. This became more clear when India recently accepted the new World Trade Organisation (WTO) accord on financial services. "We are happy that an agreement has been reached to open up financial services," said Indian Commerce Secretary P. P. Prabhu.[7]

As per the agreement India has to allow the opening up of 12 branches of foreign banks in a year as against 8 at present. Besides, the U.S. is likely to put pressure on India to open up the insurance sector in the future. At the U.S. Investment Summit held in India in December 1997, both the U.S. investors as well as government representatives made it clear that the opening up of India's insurance sector is the key prerequisite for attracting foreign investment flows to the country.

With pressure coming up from domestic and international market players to further open up financial markets, the Indian government is quickly giving up policy instruments which would allow it to exercise some degree of control over private capital flows. This has wider economic, social and political ramifications in the long run.

References

1. See, for instance, Bishwajit Bhattacharyya, "Rupee: Falling or Felled," *The Economic Times,* December 18, 1997.

2. "When Giants Meet," editorial in the *Business Standard*, December 18, 1997.

3. Deepali Srivastava, "Broken Masters of the Universe," *Business Standard*, December 13, 1997.

4. Aziz Jahangir, *Discretionary Trading and Asset Price Volatility*, IMF Working Paper No. 95/104, International Monetary Fund, October 1995.

5. "India's Best Bank," FE-BRIS Survey 1997, *Financial Express*, December 1997.

6. *Ibid.*

7. Quoted in "India Hails Accord," *Indian Express*, December 14, 1997.

PART III

Policy Implications and Interventions

What is the nature of hot money flows and how these undermine the economy is the subject of discussion in the first chapter of this section. How these flows undermine the power of the nation-state is also dealt with.

The importance of and possible regulations and controls over global financial flows in both developed and developing countries are discussed in the next chapter.

The last chapter, in this part, argues for mass action to achieve social control over global capital flows. It provides information resources consisting of like-minded researchers, research and documentation centres and campaign groups active on issues related to globalisation of finance.

10

Emerging Economic and Political Issues

Undermining of National Economies

THE recent surge in hot money flows, especially in the context of developing countries, clearly points to the fact that these flows significantly contribute to the emergence of crisis-like situations in developing countries. This has become evident through the currency crises in Mexico in 1994, and in the Southeast Asian countries in 1997. Being speculative in nature and extremely volatile, these flows can bring sharp swings in exchange rates and current account balances. Even developed countries cannot protect themselves from the vagaries of finance capital. For instance, a similar pressure on the pound occurred in 1992, and speculators were able to overpower central banks and force a devaluation. A few months later, another wave of speculative attack forced the EMU to widen the ERM in order to accomodate the French franc, which had badly depreciated out of the earlier band. Thus, the argument put forward by the IFIs and others that such flows contribute to stabilisation and are likely to help economies is contradicted by these recent experiences.

Portfolio flows, in the form of bank loans or acquisitions of bonds and stocks, pose their own problems both at corporate and national levels. At the corporate level, although these flows can offer an easier route to raise foreign capital rather than seeking it through an FDI partner, they remain highly unstable. Since portfolio securities are normally traded in secondary markets, these investors can get out of an investment relatively easily, as compared with direct investment. Because of liquidity more capital will come in, but it will try to escape, thereby depressing prices. Even new issues may not contribute to additional investment if the proceeds are used to retire other domestic debt or fund current expenditures or are mobilised for speculative purposes by the company. Thus, it will be wrong to assume that all portfolio investments bring in new capital or create socially valuable investment.

At the national level, hot money flows can contribute to currency appreciation and accumulation of foreign exchange reserves. They can lead to significant asset inflation, and thus tend to reduce domestic savings rather than increase investment. The experience of Mexico coupled with recent studies clearly show that finance capital does not always contribute to the growth of the national savings. Analysts have pointed out that the hike in interest rates to attract finance capital increases the cost of financing productive investments, which adversely affects new investments in the productive sectors of the economy. Besides, the fact that finance capital has largely been used to serve consumption, rather than investment and growth, is undeniable.

Furthermore, it has been well documented that there has been an increase in the volatility of flows as countries integrate their financial markets with global finance capital. As many countries have removed curbs to attract finance capital, the threat of major reversals of flows looms large. In the recent past, a number of developing countries have seen such reversals: Turkey and Venezuela were the first to experience major capital reversals in the 1990s, followed by Mexico in 1994, and the Southeast Asian countries in 1997. In the Mexican and the Southeast Asian cases, the contagion effect of reversals was also experienced by many neighbouring countries. Given that the price volatility of financial markets of the developing countries is higher than in developed countries, the impacts of reversals are also very severe.

Other factors contribute to the reversals of flows, irrespective of the economic fundamentals. Factors such as 'herd instinct' and contagion effect are major contributors in the reversals of flows, even if economic fundamentals of the economy are strong. In such a scenario, investors are unlikely to make any investment, although it may be highly profitable. Given the fact that investors are more susceptible to herd behaviour, the decision taken by a few institutional investors to sell their stocks can lead to sudden selling of stocks by other investors, thereby creating panic in the markets. In the case of developing countries, where financial markets are quite small as compared to developing countries and the FIIs command a dominant position, the role of herding behaviour in creating volatility, and thereby instability, in these markets cannot be overlooked.

The cost of instability is paid by the country and people at large, while currency traders and speculators tend to benefit from instability in the currency markets. Over the years, the costs of running currency business has increased, and the only way the traders and speculators can maximise the profits is by a high turnover of business. High turnovers are likely to happen when the markets are volatile and unstable. In the words of analysts at Salomon Brothers, "Logically, the most destabilising environment for an institutional house is a relatively stagnant rate environment." Thus, these international players along with their domestic counterparts benefit when these flows move in, and they even benefit when these flows threaten to move out.

Globalisation versus Nation-State

Very few will dispute the fact that the bargaining power of finance capital has been enhanced and the relative autonomy of states is being increasingly reduced, especially in the past decade. Despite growing political protest at the grass root level in many countries, the process of globalisation continues unabated because the counter-forces still lack a clearly articulated action programme and unity. The financial integration of developing countries is bound to deepen and broaden in the coming years and financial flows to developing countries as well as among developing countries themselves and from developing to developed countries will rise substantially.

The consequences of the globalisation of finance on the nation-state are substantial. The recent experiences in Southeast Asia and Latin America indicate that hot money flows can be disruptive and that governments should take strong action. But the growing globalisation of finance has led to rapid decline in the degree of control and manoeuvrability of national governments, which find it extremely difficult to intervene to reduce the volatility and establish stability in the financial markets. On macro-economic policy matters too, the governments are finding it difficult to pursue independent policies which may be inconsistent with the interests of global capital. A decade or so back, national governments in both developing and developed countries to an extent were able to pursue domestic economic management through fiscal and monetary policies. Given the fact that presently the main concern of the political leadership in both developing and developed countries is largely to seek foreign capital, the governments have shifted their efforts away from growth via monetary and fiscal policy. They are more concerned with adopting policies that are consistent with the investment priorities of global capital, and therefore do not find it possible to take steps that might lead holders of liquid capital to shift their funds to other countries offering higher interest rates and better returns.

In matters related to tax collection and evasion, the globalisation of finance has made it difficult for countries to deal with it. As countries are offering liberal concessions to foreigners (including residents of neighbouring countries) in order to attract foreign capital, the list of countries soliciting business as 'tax havens' has increased, and evasion of tax has become easier in recent years. In such a situation, the governments have very few alternatives but to reduce the tax rates in order to avoid capital flight. As a result, there is increased competitiveness among the countries to attract finance capital by offering a liberal regulatory framework and tax concessions. The recent experiences in many countries show that there are no substantial differences in the policies towards finance capital whether the governments in power are left or right. This point is well illustrated by a recent statement of a foreign banker on the possibility of the right-wing Bhartiya Janata Party coming into power in India, "We are reconciled to any colour of government at New Delhi. Only, we want the colour to hold fast. International investors have been quite comfortable with Red China."[1]

Even the developed countries find it difficult to intervene in the foreign exchange markets because their reserves are now inadequate to influence exchange rates. For instance, in 1983 the foreign exchange reserves of the largest industrial countries were more than double the level of daily foreign exchange trading. By 1995 exchange trading was double the level of reserves. Besides, the growing integration of the securities companies with banking institutions in many developed countries poses the problem of a potential crisis because the securities business is more risky and less regulated as compared to banking. Thus, a large crisis can emerge if there is a shock in the securities market, which will spread to the banks and thereby to the entire financial system. Thanks to the globalisation of financial markets, financial shocks can get easily transmitted across borders, thereby creating financial crises on the global level.

The state and its agencies are no longer the most important actors in the global economic system; they have been replaced by the TNCs. Even the analysis of many economic indicators on the basis of the nation-state is increasingly becoming obsolete. For instance, trade between nations can no longer be described as the exchange of goods produced by each nation. Nowadays, a large volume of trade is conducted as intra-firm and inter-firm trade among TNCs.

Globalisation and 'Democracy' Promotion

By reducing the ability of nation-states to intervene in economic spheres, globalisation has led to the creation of a world-wide polarisation between a rich minority and a poor majority, both in the North and the South. The conflicts between elites of the North and the South have been contained, while poverty has become a global phenomenon, increasingly prevalent in both absolute and relative forms. With the emergence of a transnational elite supported by supranational institutions such as the IMF, World

Bank and WTO, the formulation of national policies is no longer carried out by the nation-states. Increasingly the policies, especially those related to economic management, are decided by the supranational institutions which are secretive and anti-democratic in their functioning with no public accountability. It needs to be reiterated here that these institutions no longer serve the interests of a particular state, but that of a transnational elite located all over the world.

However, this does not mean that the nation-state will disappear. The transnational elite still require the state to perform those functions which provide stability to it. This includes providing macro-economic stability and, more importantly, ensuring social and political stability. As social and political conflict and unrest are likely to emerge with increasing globalisation, states will take on repressive measures to deal with them. But we may not witness dictatorships or authoritarianism as happened in the past. Under the new global setting, 'democracy' seems to have replaced the earlier preference of supporting dictatorships in the third world countries. The reasons for this are obvious - the experiences in Philippines and Chile, and recently in Indonesia, clearly show that dictators can cause serious political instability. As all sections of the deprived population tend to join hands to oust dictators, such mobilisation of the masses can also lead to major reversals in policies thereby adversely affecting the interests of the transnational elite. In the words of George Soros, "One thing is certain: Political instability is not conducive to investment."[2] On the other hand, the political system under formal 'democracy' pre-empts any radical political and economic change and preserves the socio-economic order. It helps in the continuation of elite-based and undemocratic political and economic structures. It has nothing to do with the promotion of democratic rights of the people and democratisation of decision making processes.

Thus, the promotion of nominal 'democracy' serves the interests of the transnational elite who control political and economic power at the global levels. This fact was very much evident in the case of Indonesia in recent months when all of a sudden a lobby consisting of TNCs, IMF, international media and political leaders, held Mr. Suharto responsible for the financial crisis in Indonesia and asked him to step down.

Surprisingly, till recently Suharto was supported by these same forces in spite of sharp criticism of his policies by various human rights, labour unions and citizens groups all over the world. A recent editorial in an important international weekly captured this point well:

> ... the man whose 32-year rule has taken Indonesia from a scattering of unstable, poverty-stricken islands to a prosperous regional power is not credible as the man who must now take it through its next stage of development. Rigidity and autocracy may have served to consolidate Indonesia; flexibility and democracy are now needed to safeguard its unity and allow its growth to continue. If Mr. Suharto was once the solution, he is now a large part of the problem... if Mr. Suharto now retires gracefully and the army sees that he is replaced by a reformer, it need not be too late to restore Indonesia's economic fortunes - and set it at last on the road to democracy.[3]

This clearly highlights the fact that the process of globalisation is contradictory and incompatible with the concept of genuine democracy, and further raises the issue that economic globalisation is being accompanied by the globalisation of legal, political and national institutions.

References

1. Quoted in P. Devarajan, "If we could choose the Finance Minister," *Business Line,* March 5, 1998.

2. George Soros, with Byron Wien and Krisztina Koenen, *Soros on Soros: Staying Ahead of the Curve*, John Wiley and Sons, 1995, p.158.

3. "Stand down, Suharto," *The Economist,* January 17, 1998.

11

Cooling Hot Money: The Need for Capital Controls

THE Mexican crisis of 1994-95 and the currency crisis of Southeast Asia in 1997 clearly revealed that global financial flows are volatile, and create economic instability. The World Bank, IMF and WTO, with the active support of the U.S. and other countries, are putting pressure on developing countries to further open up their financial services sectors and move towards full capital account convertibility. With the signing of the WTO agreement on financial services in December 1997, global financial flows are going to witness a boom in the coming years. Unfortunately, the developing countries are following these diktats, and are pursuing policies to open up the financial markets and remove restrictions on capital inflows and outflows.

These recent and ongoing crises have given rise to serious debates on how to control economic instability. The need for greater regulation of capital flows is expressed even by George Soros, a major player in the financial markets. He has advocated a new international mechanism to regulate financial markets as the existing IFIs have failed to do so.

Why Regulations are Essential?

It is increasingly being acknowledged that unless proper regulatory control mechanisms are developed, we shall continue to witness greater financial turmoil in the world. To minimise or eliminate the growing risks for the global financial system as a whole as well as for the individual investors, capital controls have become necessary. We are certainly not advocating a return to the types of regulations that existed in the 1960s and 1970s; but we very much need new types of regulations that are appropriate for the needs of the new global financial system of the 1990s resulting largely from deregulation.

There is a greater need for and role of official supervision and regulation in a true free market economy, as the dangers of business failures are much higher than in a closed economy. And these failures are bound to have a serious impact on the financial institutions which lend to the business sector. What may be profitable and, therefore, desirable to a private actor in the financial markets may not be sustainable and viable for a country's macro-economic policies. Hence, there is a greater need for government monitoring, supervision and regulation of private flows in a global world.

Regulations indeed become very necessary when a country is opening up for global capital inflows. When the new financial flows are increasing, many private lenders and borrowers may assume, based on past experiences in Mexico and Southeast Asia, that there are government guarantees on their flows as governments will intervene at a later stage to bail out the private sector at taxpayers' expense if things go wrong. As financial markets are more prone to overreact in both directions through a 'herd instinct,' this can cause severe costs to society and economy. To avoid such a situation of market failure to emerge, there is a greater need for regulation and supervision.

We have often been told that there are no effective mechanisms to regulate and control capital flows, and the task should be left to the markets to control themselves on the principle of self-discipline. Any controls on capital movements are opposed. It is argued that the market is the best tool for determining how money should be invested; if capital is allowed to move freely, markets will reward countries that pursue sound economic policies and pressure the rest to do the same. But the recent financial crises in Mexico and Southeast Asian countries show that these countries were following market-friendly policies, and yet they were punished by the same market forces. In the words of Malaysian Prime Minister Mahathir Mohamed,

> A world trading system cannot rely entirely on market forces... since the beginning of time, market forces by themselves have been exploitative.[1]

The history clearly shows that the markets have failed in controlling themselves, while the costs of market failures have been paid for by the society at large.

Monitoring Financial Flows

To have any effective controls over global capital flows, it is essential to have regular monitoring at both the national and global levels. Past experience shows that insufficient information can lead to incorrect policy-making and controls. Unfortunately, there is hardly any one reliable source of information on these flows. Both the home countries and the host countries lack precise information on the nature and status of these flows.

The recent growth of global institutional investors implies that these flows are completely unregulated in their source country. There is lack of sufficient disclosure of many flows. Although the IMF has suggested that there should be greater surveillance of recipient countries, it has not advocated surveillance of developed countries from where these flows originate. Thus, there is an urgent need for regulatory restrictions on investors by home country regulators, otherwise restrictions in the recipient countries will remain futile.

Given the fact that a large number of developing countries have recently opened up their financial markets to global capital, the regular recording and reporting of data in these countries is very weak. At the international level, one expects from international institutions such as the

BIS and the IMF to carefully monitor these flows but they have failed to do so effectively. There is no doubt that the monitoring of global capital flows is not an easy task, as these are global in nature, and investments are made through a variety of instruments. Thus, it becomes very difficult to include or omit a particular transaction. Besideš, there are many methodological problems, such as calculating effective yields on bonds or accounting offshore issuing activities. Relevant timely and independent data will help the regulators to adopt a particular set of policies to deal with a particular type of flow.

There is a need for exchange of data among the regulatory bodies for banking, securities and other sectors. This information should be regularly shared among countries and international institutions in order to collectively respond to emerging issues.

Policy Mechanisms

Over the years, various mechanisms to regulate and control financial flows at both international and national levels have been suggested, and many of these have been successfully implemented in some countries including Chile and Columbia. But owing to the lack of political will on the part of governments and international financial institutions, these mechanisms have not received enough attention. Some of these measures to regulate capital flows at the global levels are summarised below.

A Global Tax (Tobin tax)

A global tax on international currency movements was first proposed by Professor James Tobin in 1972. Since the Nobel Laureate James Tobin was the first to propose this tax it is also called as Tobin tax. Tobin advocated this tax as a way of discouraging speculation in short-term foreign exchange dealings, and thus minimising shocks from large currency movements. The idea was mooted to control volatility of the international currency markets and to preserve some autonomy in national currency policies.[2]

Tobin's proposal is for a 1/4 percent tax on currency transactions. Under the proposal, the tax would slow down speculative, short-term capital flows, as they will be taxed every time they cross the borders, while it will have only a marginal effect on long-term flows. Since many other transactions are taxed in some form or other, the absence of taxing on-the-spot transactions in foreign exchange acts as a strong incentive for speculators to operate in this market rather than in others. Thus, the cost of the Tobin tax for longer-term investors would be negligible, and such a tax would not interfere with genuine investments.

The Tobin tax proposal does not aim at creating a supranational taxation power. Instead, governments would levy the tax nationally. The proposal requires an agreement between at least the major financial centre countries to levy the tax at the same rate on all private spot and forward forex transactions made within their jurisdiction, including transactions in Eurocurrency other than the home currency.

Given the volatility of short-term flows, the Tobin tax serves as perhaps the best instrument to discourage short-term flows. Although the idea needs to be updated, modified and debated in the present context, nevertheless, it does offer an attractive proposition to deal with many issues related to the volatility and instability of global financial flows. Many analysts have argued that it could be introduced on a temporary basis for a fixed period, for e.g., 5-7 years. This would be consistent with the fairly widespread perception that financial fragility and systemic risk are particularly high in the current stage of transition from regulated to deregulated financial markets.

Another advantage of the Tobin tax is that it would increase the autonomy of national authorities in formulating monetary and macro-economic policy, and create a measure of insulation from the effects of international money markets. Such an autonomy would be particularly valuable for third world countries as they are more vulnerable to external capital flows.

Moreover, the Tobin tax is also desirable from the point of view of its revenue potential. It can generate forex reserves which can be used during the period of currency flight. Its counterpart domestic currency and financial resources can be used for the removal of poverty, hunger, environmental degradation, illiteracy, etc. The revenue potential of a 0.25 percent tax in the 1970s was relatively modest; with the 1995 global forex volume, annual revenue raised would be closer to $300 billion. This amount is very tempting given the fact that international official aid is declining over the years, and the national governments are faced with less financial resources for social sector spending due to the implementation of structural adjustment programmes.

An additional advantage of the tax is that it could facilitate the monitoring of international financial flows by providing a centralised data base on such flows which is badly needed. This could be particularly valuable to developing countries where large information gaps exist.

Given the fact that the tax would certainly be progressive, as there would be a shift of resources from the players in financial markets, mainly situated in industrial countries, towards the developing countries, it has not received support from the G-7 countries, international banks, the World Bank and the IMF. The critics of Tobin tax argue that it is impossible to get all countries to agree to a common tax. But a beginning can be made with a few countries coming together if it is not possible in the near future to enlist the support of all countries. For instance, a small Tobin tax could be instituted by agreement among the seven major centres of currency trading, namely, the U.S., U.K., Japan, Singapore, Switzerland, Hong Kong and Germany, where 80 percent of all currency transactions takes place. An agreement among the seven countries to levy and supervise the collection of tax is feasible. This would also contain the threat of relocation of funds, as the various island heavens are mere booking addresses that function because the mainland authorities have tolerated such evasive tactics.

The idea of Tobin tax has certainly generated a lot of interest among many economists, NGOs, trade unions and political groups all over the world. This became very evident during the World Social Summit in 1995, when many social groups and movements advocated the imposition of Tobin tax to raise additional resources to finance developmental projects.

To be sure, not all problems related to global finance can be solved by the imposition of the Tobin tax , but it can certainly serve as a first step towards developing a more stable global financial system. It can be followed up by other policy measures to achieve that purpose. Perhaps, the Tobin tax is the only scheme on which much work has already been done. What we need is the strong political will to put it into action.

A Cross-Border Payments Tax

Another mechanism, quite similar to the Tobin tax proposal, has been put forward by Rudi Dornbusch, who suggested that even without an international agreement (which is required under the Tobin tax), a cross-border payments tax by each country can help in the domestication of capital flows, without affecting the capital investments.[3] Under this scheme, the cross-border payments tax would manage the pace of cross-border flows and would fall completely within the jurisdiction of the country levying it. Every sale or purchase of foreign exchange and every cross-border payment, under the proposal, will be taxed at the rate of 0.25 percent - whether it be a goods transaction, a service deal or a financial operation. This tax proposal deals more with current account rather than with capital transactions.

Tax on Short-Term Profits

Two significant alternative proposals have been suggested recently to reduce currency speculation. J. Melitz has proposed that a 100 percent levy should be imposed on foreign-exchange profits in positions held for less than one year, while no tax deduction should be imposed on losses.[4] Similarly, in the case of stock trading, Warren Buffet has proposed that all gains from the sale of stocks or derivative securities held for less than a year should be subject to the 100 percent tax.[5]

Enforcement of Capital Controls by National Governments

The problems of volatility and instability of large capital flows have led to various policy responses from the governments. Although the global trend is towards the gradual softening of inward and outward investment restrictions and removal of capital controls, yet many countries in the recent past have adopted policy measures at one time or the other to slow them down. (See Box 11.1). The nature and impacts of these controls differ from country to country depending on the composition of the inflows and other specific conditions of each country. However, the most concerted and sustained efforts at constraining capital inflows

Box 11.1
Capital Controls in Developing Countries

Category	Number of Countries Maintaining Controls
Any form of capital control	119
Comprehensive controls	67
On outflows	67
On inflows	17
Foreign direct investments	107
Of non-residents	84
Of residents	35
Profit repatriation and capital liquidation	34
Taxes on capital transactions	9
Non-resident-controlled enterprises	6
Portfolio investments	61
Of non-residents	30
Of residents	33
Security issuance by non-residents	15
Security issuance abroad by residents	6
Debt-to-equity conversion	2
Financial transactions	78
Of non-residents	41
Of residents	66
Trade-related financial transactions	7
Deposit requirements for borrowing from abroad by residents	2
Deposit accounts	83
Of non-residents in foreign exchange	37
Of non-residents in local currency	52
Of residents abroad	29
Of residents in foreign currency with domestic banks	23
Other capital transfers	70
Personal capital transfers	34
Blocked accounts	24
Real estate transactions of non-residents	23
Of residents	30

Source : Quirk, Peter J., Owen Evans, et. al,*Capital Account Convertibility, Review of Experience and Implications for IMF Policies*, Occasional Paper 131, IMF, Washington D.C., October 1995.

were made by Chile. In other cases, many countries continued existing controls in the wake of new capital flows. Annex E enlists the controls related to restrictions on foreign investments or foreign exchange movements in emerging equity markets. As compared to Latin America, controls are more in Asia. However, the recent experience shows that these controls have been more successful in the Latin American countries (e.g. Chile and Columbia) in comparison with Asia.

Capital Controls in Chile

Chile is one country which has successfully implemented capital controls. In 1991 Chile introduced controls on capital inflows in the form of minimum non-remunerated reserve requirements of 20 percent on new foreign credits with maturities of less than one year. In simple terms, it

Box 11.2

Main Policy Responses to Capital Inflows 1988-95

	New restrictions on inflows	Liberalisa- tion of outflows	Sterilised inter- vention	Higher reserve requirements
East Asia				
Indonesia	1991		1990-93	
Korea		1989-94	1989,1992-93	1990
Malaysia	1992, 1994	1988-94	1992-93	1989-92, '94
Philippines		1992,1994-95	1990-93	1990
Thailand	1995	1990-94	1988-95	
Latin America				
Brazil	1993-95		1994-95	
Chile	1991-93	1990-94	1990,1992-93	1992
Colombia	1993-95	1991-94	1992-95	1991
Mexico	1992	1991	1990-93	
South Asia				
India	1992-95	ongoing	1993-94	1993-94
Pakistan		ongoing	1993-94	
Sri Lanka	1993	1993	1991-93	1991-93

Source : *Private Capital Flows to Developing Countries*, World Bank, 1997.

meant that local firms in Chile which borrow from abroad must keep 20 percent of that loan on deposit at the central bank - without interest - for a year. Even the loan is for a shorter duration.

In 1992, the 20 percent reserve requirement on foreign loans was extended to foreign currency bank deposits. In May 1992 the required reserve ratio was further increased to 30 percent. In July 1995 the reserve requirements were extended to all types of foreign investments in Chile, including the issue of secondary American depository receipts.

These controls have helped Chile in many ways. Firstly, it discouraged short-term and speculative foreign capital inflows as these became expensive. Secondly, long-term capital inflows increased as these measures encouraged firms to borrow for long-term purposes. Analysts have found that these controls led to major changes in the composition of inflows, from short-term to long-term periods without adversely affecting the overall volume of the capital inflows.

Thanks to these controls, the impact of the Mexican crisis of 1994 on the Chilean financial markets was almost negligible, while other countries in the region were badly affected by it. In fact, the stable external financial position coupled with strong economic fundamentals enabled Chile to become the first country in the entire Latin American region to obtain an investment rating of A- by Standard and Poor's in 1995.

Chile also took another significant policy measure to increase its domestic saving base through the development of a private pension saving system. This helped in two ways: it helped Chile to finance most of its needs domestically and, more importantly, it reduced the vulnerability of its domestic financial system in the event of sudden outflows of capital, which had happened in the case of Mexico. Recently, Colombia has also followed the Chilean policy measures to control foreign capital inflows.

Thus, the argument that controls could lead to contraction of capital inflows carries little weight in the light of the Chilean experience, which clearly demonstrates that countries can attract a significant volume of capital inflows, despite imposition of controls to keep off short-term speculative inflows.

Box 11.3
The Central Banking System

The central banks in the countries have the function of monitoring and regulating the country's monetary and financial systems. They try to regulate the value of the country's currency at home and in the international market. The bank issues currency and may trade gold or other currencies in exchange for its own. It also holds some form of money in reserve that it can use in making international transactions. With the globalisation of finance, central banks also cooperate with each other to protect the stability of the world's currencies. In certain countries the central banks are still very much linked with the government, while the global trend is towards giving more autonomy to the central banks. In fact, the IMF insists on giving more freedom to the central banks and in a few countries it has succeeded in putting its own nominees to head the central banks. Generally, a country has one central bank, for instance, Reserve Bank of India, in India. In some countries, there is more than one central bank, for instance, in the U.S., the Federal Reserve System has 12 separate banks around the nation, each with its own directors. The system is governed by a seven-member Federal Reserve Board, located at Washington.

Following is the list of central banks in Asia:

Australia Reserve Bank of Australia

Bangladesh Bangladesh Bank

Burma Union Bank of Burma

Cambodia National Bank of Cambodia

China People's Bank of China

Fiji Reserve Bank of Fiji

Hong Kong The Monetary Authority of Hong Kong is the *de facto* central bank

India Reserve Bank of India

Indonesia Bank Indonesia

Japan Bank of Japan

Laos Banque d'Etat de la RDP Lao

Malaysia Bank Negara Malaysia

Maldives The Maldives Monetary Authority

Nepal Nepal Rastra Bank

New Zealand Reserve Bank of New Zealand

Papua New Guinea Bank of Papua New Guinea

Pakistan State Bank of Pakistan

Philippines Central Bank of the Philippines

Singapore The Monetary Authority of Singapore is the *de facto* central bank

Solomon Islands The Solomon Islands Monetary Authority

South Korea Bank of Korea

Sri Lanka Bank of Ceylon

Thailand Bank of Thailand

Vietnam State Bank of Vietnam

Capital Controls in other Countries

Pakistan is the only country in the Asian region (and perhaps among the developing countries) which has not introduced capital controls, while all other countries in the region have different kinds of controls in place. Of late, Korea and Taiwan, which had imposed strict controls in the form of registration procedures and investment ceilings, started implementing these controls from 1996 onwards.

On the other hand, countries in Latin America undertook controls largely to avert sudden capital outflows. Experiencing an outflow of about $8 billion in 1995, Argentina established a stand-by financing facility of more than $6 billion to avert such a crisis in the future. Mexico and Chile have introduced new policy measures which give more flexibility to the central banks to intervene in the currency markets. Chile adjusted the band within which its currency floats, in order to allow for further appreciation of the peso. Similarly, many countries in Latin America have also introduced a set of taxes (e.g. capital gains tax) and regulatory mechanisms to manage the inflows.

On the other hand, countries where the inflows were mostly portfolio investments, a variety of controls have been introduced in the form of restrictions on the domestic companies' access to international markets as well as on acquisition of domestic companies by the foreigners. For instance, in Brazil, aggregate foreign ownership is limited to 49 percent of a listed company's voting shares (100 percent of non-voting shares), 25 percent in Chile, 49 percent in Indonesia, 20 percent in Korea, 24 percent in India, 40 percent in the Philippines, and 15 to 65 percent in Thailand, depending on the sector. Another form of restriction was used to limit the domestic firms' issuance of securities abroad in countries such as Chile and India. In Chile only securities rated by a domestic rating agency can be placed abroad. In India, the domestic companies interested in raising securities abroad are restricted through a ceiling on the maximum limits of borrowings. In Brazil limits on minimum maturities of bonds have been imposed from time to time.

Besides, in some countries (for e.g. in India), the authorities have introduced capital gains tax to reduce short-term flows, while many countries have imposed financial transaction taxes on foreign purchases

Box 11.4

Exchange Rate Systems

CURRENCY BOARD A currency board is a monetary authority which fixes a currency to an anchor currency (usually dollar or German mark) at a specific rate, thereby eliminating the uncertainties of a floating currency. Under this system, every unit of local currency in circulation is supposed to be backed by the foreign currency. However, under this arrangement, a country loses all its autonomy and flexibility to pursue monetary policies, as it cannot set interest rates or inject liquidity into the economy. The exchange rate is immutable and everything else becomes variable.

DIRTY FLOAT   Occurs when governments attempt to influence exchange rates to prevent extreme changes in exchange rates which are otherwise flexible and allowed to float. Also called a *managed float*.

EXCHANGE RATE MECH-ANISM (ERM) The procedure used for fixing exchange rates within the European Monetary System from 1979 to 1993. The ERM involved establishing a grid which provided upper and lower support points for each member's currency versus every other member's currency. When an exchange rate between two currencies approached a support point, the central banks of both countries were required to take action.

FIXED EXCHANGE RATES A system of exchange rate determination in which governments try to maintain exchange rates at selected official levels.

FLEXIBLE EXCHANGE RATES A system of exchange rates in which the rates are determined by the forces of supply and demand without any intervention by governments or official bodies.

PEGGED EXCHANGE RATES Another term for *fixed exchange rates*, which are rates set by governments at selected, official levels.

STERILIZATION POLICY A policy of not allowing changes in foreign exchange reserves to affect a country's money supply, frustrating the automatic price-adjustment mechanism. Also called *neutralization policy*.

WIDER BAND   A compromise between fixed and flexible exchange rates which allows exchange rates to fluctuate by a relatively large amount on either side of an official value.

of domestic bonds in 1993, and on purchases of domestic stocks in 1994.

At the same time, many developing countries have also introduced a series of macro-economic measures from time to time to manage capital flows which include interventions in the currency markets through sterilised intervention and different exchange rate systems (e.g. pure floating, managed or dirty floating, fixed exchange rate, currency board, etc.). Although many of these measures have not been successful as the recent Southeast Asian crisis shows, still they present a wide range of controls which exist within the arena of national authorities.

The past experiences with these policy instruments bring out the point that it is not undesirable and impossible to have controls over private capital flows. In fact, with more and more countries opening their financial markets to private capital flows, there is an urgent need

---

Box 11.5

The Bank for International Settlements is the world's oldest international financial institution, having been in operation since 1930. Located in Basle, Switzerland, BIS is an organisation of central banks and bank regulators. It serves as a forum for central bankers to discuss international regulatory standards and coordinate central bank policies. Consisting of central banks from developed countries, nearly all the European central banks as well as those of the U.S., Canada, Japan, Australia and South Africa are associated with the activities of the BIS. Operating under its auspices, the Basle Committee proposed guidelines for the measurement and assessment of the capital adequacy of banks operating globally. In 1988, these guidelines were accepted by the Group of Ten countries and the agreement was known as Basle Accord. However, the closure of the Bank for Credit and Capital International (BCCI) in 1991 exposed the shortcomings of the Basle Accord.

The International Organisation of Securities Commissions (IOSCO) is an association of securities market regulatory bodies (e.g. SEBI in India) at the international level. The organisation has 134 members. The main purpose of IOSCO is to promote standardised practices across the world to facilitate better supervision by regulators. It also provides opinions on matters related to market regulation through its various committees.

for effective and appropriate kinds of controls depending on the nature of these flows as well as the country's financial markets.

Apart from national controls, the need for a regional and international supervision and regulation of global capital flows is in tune with the global nature of these flows. Unfortunately, the present trend is towards increasing deregulation and relaxation of existing controls, especially in the developing world. It seems that policy-makers have not learnt any lessons from the experiences of the Mexican and Southeast Asian crises. An important issue which remains unanswered is who should take the initiative. In recent years, national governments in developing countries (e.g. Chilean government) have taken policy initiatives. But greater efforts are required at the regional and international levels. With the failure of IFIs, especially the IMF, organisations such as the BIS and IOSCO have taken over the task of coordinating such regulations at the global level. But recent events, such as the collapse of BCCI and the Southeast Asian currency crises, show that these institutions are largely ineffective, and better mechanisms are needed to specifically deal with these issues.

However, in the absence of a broader citizens' initiative to exert social control over finance capital, such mechanisms will remain ineffective both at the national and international levels.

References

1   "Asian Currency Woes Fuel Debate in Controlling Global Capital Flow," *Indian Express*, November 10, 1997.

2   For a detailed discussion on this proposal see, M. Haq, I. Kaul and I. Grunberg (eds.), *The Tobin Tax: Coping with Financial Volatility*, Oxford University Press, 1996.

3   See R. Dornbusch, "Cross-Border Payments Taxes and Alternative Capital Account Regimes," paper prepared for the Group of 24, 1995, UNCTAD, *International Monetary and Financial Issues for the 1990s, Research Papers for the Group of Twenty-Four*, Vol. VIII, 1997.

4   J. Melitz, "Comment on the Tobin Tax," CIDEI Working Paper, 1994.

5   Concerning Buffet's proposal see L. Lowenstein, *What's Wrong with Wall Street? Short-Term Gain and the Absentee Shareholder*, Addison-Wesley, 1988.

12

Resources for Action

CITIZENS can play an important role in protecting economies from the onslaught of global finance. The South Korean case has demonstrated this, where people raised nearly $20 billion by voluntarily contributing their personal gold belongings. However, until and unless the people are organised to make both the national and international players accountable and responsive, such actions may finally end up providing band-aid rather than bringing about structural changes in the global financial system.

Despite the information gap, the complex issue of global finance is increasingly getting the attention of various individuals and groups involved in social action. With the decline of trade unions and the acceptance of a neo-liberal agenda by governments in power irrespective of their colour, many social movements are passing through a phase of isolation and inertia. Thus, they are finding it extremely difficult to challenge the globalisation process.

For any social action to yield the desired results in the present economic and political environment, we may have to rethink our traditional strategies. Perhaps, social movements need new tools of action as they face new challenges and obstacles. Although the campaign strategies and tools will differ from country to country, yet a number of common factors should be taken into account.

Firstly, campaigns should have a cross-sectoral mass base consisting of groups and individuals belonging to different socio-economic, cultural and political backgrounds. Given the fact that it is always beneficial to broaden the support base, a common minimum programme can be worked out which is acceptable to all constituents. Secondly, to mobilise vast sections of the population requires educational and awareness building campaigns and effective use of various kinds of media. Popular educational tools such as pamphlets, primers, comic books, audio-video materials and street theatre can play an important role in achieving this objective. Thirdly, since information on these issues is rarely accessible and whatever is available is highly technical, the campaigns should have the support of economists, intellectuals and technical experts who can regularly analyse and feed information to the campaigns. Similarly, the campaigns ought to seek the support of research and documentation institutes. Fourthly, a concrete alternative programme is needed to reinforce the fact that there are alternatives to globalisation. Without articulating any viable alternative, the campaigns run the risk of political stagnation. Since the issues are global, alternatives should also go beyond national boundaries. Fifthly, although the nation-state will remain the practical arena of struggle, the campaigns should also have an important component of transborder alliances to link up with popular movements in other countries and advocate a concrete alternative programme with common features.

Finally, campaigns need to work towards the democratisation of national governments and IFIs. But this may not be enough. The other major players in global finance such as transnational banks, institutional investors, currency traders and speculators, who have remained outside the public scrutiny, should be made accountable to the public.

Box 12.1
Campaign Against Narmada Bonds

When the campaign against the Sardar Sarovar Project (SSP) forced the World Bank to withdraw its funding to the project in March 1993, the project authorities decided to raise money through issuance of bonds in the Indian financial markets. For the Narmada Bachao Andolan (NBA)- the group leading the campaign - this was a new challenge, for we were dealing with new institutions and new concepts and it meant learning many new things. The NBA decided to oppose these bonds and launch a campaign with the message that supporting the bonds was supporting destruction. Of course, the Government of Gujarat had launched a big advertisement campaign in the print and electronic media, and the NBA's resources were no match for their budget. So the NBA took help of other means. It brought out a detailed leaflet on the bonds issue, highlighting why the people should not support the project. The NBA sent out letters to many brokers. More importantly, the NBA had a series of meetings with influential groups of investors who were likely to invest in these bonds.

NBA's campaign certainly had an impact - even though the bonds were oversubscribed. Although the authorities claimed that investors had endorsed the project by putting their money into the bonds, this was not true. Investors had nothing to do with the project. They, like any other investor, were primarily concerned with the attractive economic returns on the bonds - which included interest rates above 18 percent, and payment of interest as well as principal guaranteed by the Gujarat Government. Despite such a lucrative offer, the State government put pressure on its officials and bodies by putting targets to raise money for the bond issue.

The success of the campaign can be gauged by the fact that after this, even though the project came out with at least three bond issues, none of them have been public issues but were only for private placement. The campaign also came up with new methods in the later period. Thus, when another bond issue was being planned in 1996, the NBA too came out with a detailed financial analysis of the project and sent it to key members of the financial media as also the credit rating agencies such as CRISIL. Ultimately, that issue was abandoned by the project. Clearly, when taking the struggle into this new field, the NBA had to learn a lot of new things. Hence, it is important for movements to study and be prepared in this regard from the beginning, thereby saving valuable time and avoiding the pitfalls we had to go through.

Shripad Dharmadhikary

Information and Campaign Resources

There are many groups and individuals working on various issues related to the globalisation process. Listed below are specifically those working on issues related to globalisation of finance.

Co-Op America

This group educates people on how their money can be used to support sustainable development; helps responsible businesses emerge and thrive; pressures irresponsible companies to adopt responsible policies. Publishes *Boycott Action News, National Green Pages* and *Socially Responsible Financial Planning Handbook.*
Address: 1612 K Street NW
Suite 600, Washington D.C. 20006, U.S.
Ph: 1-202 8725307

European Campaign on Debt and Development (EURODAD)

EURODAD is a network of European NGOs from 16 countries working on issues related to debt, structural adjustment and the accountability of the Bretton Woods institutions. It organises conferences, publishes regular updates and campaigns on these issues. It has launched a campaign on the HIPC debt initiative. EURODAD is also involved in issues related to private capital flows. It recently brought out a paper titled, *The Next Crisis? Direct and Portfolio Investment in Developing Countries* by David Woodward.
Contact: Ted van Hees
Address: Rue Dejoncker 46,
1060 Brusssels, Belgium
Ph: 32-2 5439060
Fax: 32-2 5440559
E-mail: eurodad@agoranet.be

Equipo Pueblo

This organisation has been actively involved in issues related to the Mexican crisis, NAFTA and economic policies. The report, *The Polarization of Mexican Society: A Grassroots View of World Bank Economic Adjustment Policies,* was co-authored by Carlos Heredia. Through *Mexico Update* it regularly provides information on the economic, political and social situation in Mexico. Besides, it brings out a bi-monthly publication, *The Other Side of Mexico.*
Contact: Mary Purcell/Carlos Heredia
Address: Francisco Field Jurado 51,
Col. Independencia, Mexico, D.F. 03630

Ph: 525 5390015
Fax: 52-5 6727453
E-mail: pueblodip@laneta.apc.org

Friends of the Earth-U.S.
The organisation has been very active on issues related to the IMF. Recently, it organised conferences on private capital flows. The organisation also lobbies securities ratings agencies to incorporate measures of sustainability into ratings criteria. It has also brought out a handbook on international project finance titled, *The Anatomy of a Deal.*
Contact: Michelle Chan/Marijke Torfs
Address: 1025 Vemont Avenue, NW
3rd Floor, Washington, D.C. 20005, U.S.
Ph: 1-202 7837400
Fax: 1-202 7830444
E-mail: foedc@igc.apc.org

Forum on Debt and Development (FONDAD)
FONDAD is an independent policy research centre established to provide policy-oriented research on North-South problems, primarily on international financial issues. Through its international network of experts and its contacts in the world of finance, FONDAD provides information and practical strategies to policy-makers and other interested groups. FONDAD has brought out many publications on global finance. The three important titles edited by its director, Jan Joost Teunissen, are - *Fragile Finance: Rethinking the International Monetary System*, 1992; *The Pursuit of Reform: Global Finance and the Developing Countries*, 1993; and *Can Currency Crises be Prevented or Better Managed?* 1996.
Contact: Jan Joost Teunissen.
Address: Noordeinde 107 A, 25 14 GE The Hague, the Netherlands
Ph: 31-70 3653820
Fax: 31-70 3463939
E-mail: Forum_FONDAD@wxs.nl

Franklin Research and Development
This is an investment advisory service offering newsletters, economic commentary and stock recommendations on socially positive companies. It rates funds, publishes *Investing for a Better World*, and offers Franklin Research's Insight service for investment professionals.
Address: 711 Atlantic Avenue, 4th Floor,
Boston, MA 02111, U.S.
Ph: 1-617 4236655

Focus on the Global South
Affiliated to Chulalongkorn University's Social Research Institute in Thailand and **Food First** in the U.S., **Focus** is involved in regional and global policy analysis, micro-macro issues linking and advocacy work. It is currently examining the Southeast Asian economic crisis from a development perspective. On this issue, its co-director, Walden Bello, recently prepared a paper titled, *Addicted to Capital: The Ten-Year High and Present-Day Withdrawal Trauma of Southeast Asia's Economies.*
Contact: Walden Bello
Address: c/o CUSRI, Chulalongkorn University
Bangkok 10330, Thailand
Ph: 66-2 2187363
Fax: 66-2 2559976
E-mail: W.Bello@focusweb.org

IBON Foundation, Inc.
Undertakes the study of socio-economic issues that confront Philippine society today, and seeks to bring this knowledge and information to the greatest number of people. Its programmes include a Databank and Research Centre and an Institute of Political Economy. It brings out publications on various issues related to TNCs and private capital flows.
Contact: Antonio A. Tujan
Address: 3rd flr. SCC Building, 4427 Int.
Old Sta. Mesa, Manila
Ph: 7132737
Fax: 7160108
E-mail: atujan@mnl.sequel.net

Institute for Policy Studies
Since 1963, the Institute for Policy Studies has been working on issues such as TNCs, peace and security, and economic and social rights. Its global economy programme provides information and research support and links researchers and activists to monitor the impact of globalisation on environment, people and economy.
Contact: John Cavanagh/Sarah Anderson
Address: 733 15th Street, NW 10th Floor
Washington D.C. 20005
Ph: 1-202 2349382
Fax: 1-202 3877915
E-mail: ipsps@igc.apc.org.

International Forum on Globalization
IFG is an international citizens' alliance which advocates equitable, democratic, and ecologically sustainable economics. It regularly organises conferences, publishes a newsletter, and campaigns against current international trade and investment agreements, TNCs, and development banks.
Contact: Jerry Mander
Address: 1555 Pacific Avenue, San Francisco,
California 94109, U.S.
Ph: 1-415 7713394
Fax: 1-415 7711121
E-mail: ifg@igc.org

Multinationals Resource Center
The center provides information support on private capital flows, especially TNCs. The center's affiliate, **Essential Information**, brings out the magazine, *Multinational Monitor*. Recently, another of its affiliate organisations, **Essential Action** along with **Friends of the Earth** has launched a moderated listserve on issues related to the IMF.
Contact: Marcia Carroll
Address: PO Box 19405
Washington, DC 20036, U.S.
Ph: 1-202 3878030
Fax: 1-202 2345176
E-mail: mrc@essential.org

Public Interest Research Group
PIRG is a research and campaign group actively involved in issues related to TNCs, IMF-World Bank policies and globalisation. Recently, it has started regular monitoring of private capital flows to India. The organisation brings out publications and organises workshops to strengthen the information base of activists and groups involved in social action.
Contact: Kavaljit Singh
Address: 142, Maitri Apartments, Plot No. 28,
Indraprastha Extension, Patparganj, Delhi - 110 092
Ph: 91-11 2432054
Fax: 91-11 2224233
E-mail: kaval@pirg.unv.ernet.in

The Development Group for Alternative Policies (DGAP)
This group has been actively involved in articulating alternative policies, especially in the context of the structural adjustment programme, NAFTA and the Mexican financial crisis. With the active support of Southern partners, it

also lobbies the World Bank and IMF and other financial institutions on policy matters. The organisation also co-ordinates the Structural Adjustment Participatory Review Initiative (SAPRI).
Contact: Doug Hellinger/Karen Hansen-Kuhn
927 Fifteenth Street, NW, 4th Floor
Washington, DC 20005, USA
Ph: 1-202 8981566
Fax: 1-202 8981612
E-mail: dgap@igc.apc.org

Third World Network
TWN is a network of international NGOs and groups working on issues of international trade, investment, and sustainable development. It brings out two regular journals, *Third World Resurgence* and *Third World Economics*, besides other publications.
Contact: Martin Khor Kok Peng
Address: 228 Macalister Road, 10400 Penang, Malaysia
Ph: 60-4 2266728
Fax: 60-4 2264505
E-mail: twn@igc.apc.org

C.P. Chandrashekhar/Jayati Ghosh/Deepak Nayyar/Prabhat Patnaik
Centre for Economic Studies and Planning
School of Social Sciences
Jawaharlal Nehru University
New Delhi 110067

Michel Chossudovsky
Professor, Department of Economics,
University of Ottawa,
Ottawa, KIN 6N5, Canada
Ph: 1-613 7892051
Fax: 1-613 7892050
E-mail: chosso@travel-net.com

Susan George
10, Rue Jean Michelez
91510 Lardy-France
Ph: 33 (0) 1 69 27 47 15
Fax: 33 (0) 1 60 82 66 68
E-mail: sgtni@globenet.org

Stephany Griffith-Jones
Senior Fellow,
Institute of Development Studies,
Sussex University,
Sussex BN1 9RE, U.K.
Ph: 41 1273 606 261
Fax: 41 1273 621 202

Edward S. Herman
Professor Emeritus of Finance,
Wharton School, University of Pennsylvania,
28, Fairview Road,
Narberth, Pa. 19072, U.S.
Ph: 1-610 6425095
Fax: 1-610 6420794
E-mail: hermane@wharton.upenn.edu

S.L. Shetty
EPW Research Foundation
C 212, Akurli Industrial Estate, Kandivli (East)
Mumbai 400 101
Ph: 91-22 8873038
Fax: 91-22 8873038
E-mail: admin@epwrf.ilbom.ernet.in

Jomo Kwame Sundaram
Faculty of Economics and Administration
University of Malaya
50603 Kuala Lumpur, Malaysia
Ph: 60-3 7593926
Fax: 60-3 7561879
E-mail: g2jomo@umcsd.um.edu.my

Dalip S. Swamy
Professor, Department of Business Economics
University of Delhi (South Campus)
Benito Juarez Road,
Dhaula Kuan, Delhi - 110 021
Ph: 91-11 6884141

Recommended Readings

In addition to the works referred to in the text, this section provides other sources of information. One may not agree with the contents of many of these publications, but they offer information which might be of use in understanding these issues.

1.   Asian Development Bank, *Asian Development Outlook*, Manila, annual.

2.   Bank of International Settlements, *Survey of Foreign Exchange Market Activity*, Basle, 1990.

3.   *Business Week*, Hong Kong, weekly.

4.   Tony Clark, *The Emergence of Corporate Rule and what to do about it*, The White Papers, No. 1, International Forum on Globalization, 1996.

5.   *Economic and Political Weekly*, Bombay, weekly.

6.   William Greider, *One World, Ready or Not: The Manic Logic of Global Capitalism*, Simon and Schuster, 1997.

7.   ICRA, *Money and Finance*, New Delhi, quarterly.

8.   IMF, *International Capital Markets,* annual.

9.   – – , *World Economic Outlook*, biannual.

10.   — and World Bank, *Finance and Development*, Washington, quarterly.

11.   Mohsin S. Khan and Carmen M. Reinhart (eds.), *Capital Flows in the APEC Region*, Occasional Paper No. 122, IMF, March 1995.

12.   Thomas D. Lairson and David Skidmore, *International Political Economy*, Harcourt Brace College Publishers, 1997.

13.   Lal Parcham and Lok Dasta, *Globalisation of Capital*, 1997.

14.   Maurice D. Levi, *International Finance*, McGraw-Hill Inc., 1996.

15.   H. R. Machiraju, *International Financial Markets and India,* Wheeler Publishing, 1997.

16.   Hans-Peter Martin and Harald Schumann, *The Global Trap: Globalization and the Assault on Democracy and Prosperity*, Zed Books, 1997.

17.   Kenneth M. Morris, Alan M. Siegel and Beverly Larson, *Guide to Understanding Money and Investing*, Dow Jones Publishing Company (Asia) Inc., 1997.

18.   Pepijn Nicolas (eds.), *World Credit Tables 1996*, EURODAD, 1996.

19.   Peter J. Quirk and Owen Evans, *Capital Account Convertibility: Review of Experience and Implications for IMF Policies*, Occasional Paper No. 131, IMF, October, 1995.

20. A. V. Rajwade, *Foreign Exchange International Finance and Risk Management*, Academy of Business Studies, New Delhi, 1996.

21. Reserve Bank of India, *Annual Report*, Bombay, annual.

22. – – , *Report on Currency and Finance*, Bombay, annual.

23. William I. Robinson, *Promoting Polyarchy: Globalization, US Intervention and Hegemony*, Cambridge University Press, 1996.

24. Uma Shashikant and Kamla Suri, *Global Portfolio Investments in Emerging Markets and India*, UTI Institute of Capital Markets, 1996.

25. *The Economist*, London, weekly.

26. UNCTAD, *Trade and Development Report*, Geneva, annual.

27. – – , *World Investment Report*, New York, annual.

28. – – , Review 1995, *International Monetary and Financial Issues for the 1990s*, Volume VIII, 1997.

29. Romesh Vaitilingam, *Guide to Using the Financial Pages*, Pitman Publishing, 1996.

30. World Bank, *Managing Capital Flows in East Asia*, 1996.

31. – – , *South Asia's Integration into the World Economy*, 1997.

32. – – , *Private Capital Flows to Developing Countries*, Oxford University Press, 1997.

33. – – , *Financial Flows and the Developing Countries*, Washington, quarterly.

34. – – , *Global Development Finance*, Washington D.C., annual.

35. – – , *World Development Report*, Washington D.C., annual.

Annexes

Annex A: Change in Degree of Financial Integration

1985-87

Country	Level	Country	Level
Korea	High	Suriname	Low
Malaysia	High	Togo	Low
Thailand	Medium +	Tanzania	Low
Cameroon	Medium +	Swaziland	Low
India	Medium	South Africa	Low
Colombia	Medium	Peru	Low
Niger	Medium	Paraguay	Low
Kenya	Medium	Sierra Leone	Low
Papua New Guinea	Medium	Senegal	Low
Indonesia	Medium	Dominican Rep.	Low
Mexico	Medium	Costa Rica	Low
Egypt	Medium	Congo	Low
Chile	Medium	Ghana	Low
Sri Lanka	Medium -	Gabon	Low
Philippines	Medium -	El Salvador	Low
Core d'Ivoire	Medium -	China	Low
Ecuador	Medium -	Benin	Low
Mauritius	Medium -	Bangladesh	Low
Morocco	Medium -	Algeria	Low
Pakistan	Medium -	Burkina Faso	Low
Nigeria	Medium -	Brazil	Low
Turkey	Medium -	Bolivia	Low
Tunisia	Medium -	Lesotho	Low
Uruguay	Medium -	Jamaica	Low
Zimbabwe	Medium -	Madagascar	Low
Argentina	Medium -	Mauritania	Low
		Mali	Low

1992-94

Country	Level	Country	Level
Thailand	High	Tunisia	Medium -
Turkey	High	Ecuador	Medium -
Brazil	High	Kenya	Medium -
Argentina	High	Cameroon	Medium -
Korea	High	Egypt	Medium -
Indonesia	High	Togo	Low
Malaysia	High	Mauritania	Low
Mexico	High	Myanmar	Low
Hungary	High	Nicaragua	Low
Ghana	High	Tanzania	Low
Chile	High	Senegal	Low
Pakistan	High	Sierra Leone	Low
Philippines	High	Venezuela	Low
Mauritius	Medium +	Niger	Low
Panama	Medium +	Nigeria	Low
Colombia	Medium +	Zambia	Low
Jamaica	Medium +	Guatemala	Low
India	Medium +	Burkina Faso	Low
Peru	Medium	Guyana	Low
Papua New Guinea	Medium	Guinea-Bissau	Low
Morocco	Medium	Gabon	Low
Zimbabwe	Medium	Costa Rica	Low
Cote d'Ivoire	Medium	Congo	Low
Uruguay	Medium	El Salvador	Low
China	Medium	Dominican Rep.	Low
Sri Lanka	Medium -	Haiti	Low
		Madagascar	Low

Source: Adapted from *Private Capital Flows to Developing Countries*, World Bank, Oxford University Press, 1997, p.18.

Annex B: Key Macroeconomic Ratios of Thailand

	1975	1985	1990	1992	1993	1994	1995	1996
Gross Domestic Investment (percentage of GDP)	26.7	28.2	41.1	39.6	40.0	41.2	43.1	43.8
Gross National Saving (percentage of GDP)	22.5	23.9	32.4	33.9	34.3	33.2	34.3	35.3
Exports (percentage of GDP)	18.7	23.4	34.1	36.5	37.5	39.1	41.5	
Imports (percentage of GDP)	-23.4	-26.2	-41.9	-41.4	-42.7	-44.9	-48.3	
Trade Balance (percentage of GDP)	-4.7	-2.8	-7.8	-5.0	-5.2	-5.8	-6.8	
Current Account Balance (percentage of GDP)	-4.2	-4.3	-8.7	-5.7	-5.6	-5.5	-7.9	-8.0
Govt's Current Budget Balance (percentage of GDP)		-0.6	7.4	6.4	6.3	7.4	7.8	
Overall Budget Surplus (percentage of GDP)		-3.7				1.7	2.5	
Total Reserve/Avg Import per month		3.6	4.8	5.5	5.9	5.7	5.4	

Source: Mihir Rakshit, "Learning and Unlearning from the Thai Currency Crisis," *Money & Finance*, Number 3, September 1997.

Annex C: Thailand's Letter of Intent to IMF

The following is the full text of the letter submitted by Finance Minister Tarrin Nimmanhaeminda and Bank of Thailand Governor Chaiyawat Wibulswasdi to Michel Camdessus, managing director of the International Monetary Fund.

Dear Mr. Camdessus

1. The new government headed by Prime Minister Chuan has reconfirmed its full commitment to the economic programme specified in the Memorandum on Economic Policy (MEP) of August 14, 1997. Indeed, the new economic team is determined to take a number of additional measures to strengthen the policy package and reinforce public confidence in the programme. Implementation of the policies specified in the MEP has been overshadowed by very difficult economic conditions in Thailand as well as in the region. Nonetheless, all of the performance criteria for end-September 1997 were met. The new government is determined to proceed rapidly with implementation.

I: Revised Macroeconomic Framework for 1997-98

2. Our programme has now to contend with a less favourable short-term macroeconomic outlook than originally anticipated . In particular, the slower return of confidence has further depreciated the exchange rate, put pressure on interest rates, and is resulting in a much sharper decline in private investment and consumption than originally anticipated. While this turn of events will imply a weaker economy in the period immediately ahead, we are confident that the determined implementation of the economic programme will establish the conditions for Thailand's economy to return to stable growth.

3. Thus, we have reassessed the key macroeconomic objectives for 1997-98. While overall growth is still expected to be positive during this period as a whole, there will be economic contraction in many sectors in the period immediately ahead. The sharper economic downturn will help dampen the effect of currency depreciation on prices, and inflation is now projected to be only slightly higher than originally programmed in spite of the much weaker baht. The external current account deficit will, also, adjust faster than originally expected, falling to 3.9 percent of GDP in 1997 and to 1.8 percent of GDP in 1998 - i.e., more than one percentage point lower than the initial programme targets. This will help offset a weaker than expected capital account.

II: Macroeconomic Policies

Fiscal Policy

4. The altered macroeconomic environment - especially the weaker economy and the large exchange rate depreciation - has eroded the setting for fiscal policy. The revenue shortfall relative to the budget for 1997-98 is now expected to be in the order of 133

billion baht (or 2 percent of GDP), much of which can be attributed to the slower pace of economic activity. Nevertheless, we are determined to maintain the fiscal goal of keeping the consolidated public sector in a surplus of one percent of GDP in 1997-98. This will ensure an orderly offset to the anticipated costs of the financial sector restructuring, while also providing a clear signal of the government's intent to implement the economic programme.

5. For this purpose, we have reinforced the fiscal programme through additional measures to ensure compliance with the fiscal goal. While we have been forced to increase our reliance on import duties, the increased duties on luxury items, and the small surcharges are temporary and consistent with our obligations to the WTO; we have committed to reverse them by end 1999, and will strive to do so earlier. Toward this end and, most importantly, to ensure an elastic and efficient tax structure in Thailand, we intend to carry out a comprehensive review of the present tax system. For this reason, we are requesting early technical assistance from the Fund.

6. The economic downturn is also likely to reduce the retained earnings of non-financial public enterprises. However, we continue to aim for a balanced financial position for this sector. Since the adoption of the programme in August, we have reviewed the investment programmes of these enterprises and curtailed lower-priority investment spending. The new expenditure limits for the public enterprises have now been announced by the National Economic and Social Development Board and adopted by the government. The principal cuts have taken place in the investment programmes of the utilities (the electricity and water authorities, the telephone company), and Thai Airways. At the same time, adjustments are being made in all utility and state enterprise charges to reflect the larger depreciation of the baht, except for bus and rail fares which continue - as provided for in the programme - to be set below costs for the time being for social reasons. Given the uncertain macroeconomic environment and its impact on budget revenues, fiscal developments have to be kept under constant review and reassessed at the time of the second programme review.

7. Wage policy continues to be supportive of the objective of minimising the impact of the depreciation of the baht on prices. The increase in the minimum wage for the year 1998 has been limited to 2-3 percent.

Monetary Policy

8. Within the framework of our flexible exchange-rate policy, monetary policy will need to play a greater role in stabilising conditions in the foreign exchange market and containing the inflationary impact of the exchange rate depreciation. This has implications for interest-rate policy as well as for the monetary programme. As part of the Bank of Thailand's resolve to maintain such a tight monetary stance, interest rates will principally be set with the objective of helping stabilise the exchange rate and restore confi-

dence in domestic financial assets. As a guide to this policy, and once the exchange market has stabilised, we intend to keep interest rates within the interest-rate range. However, until the foreign exchange stabilises, we will be keeping short-term interest rates above this range, as necessary, in order to help stabilise the exchange market, and we will continue to use interest rates flexibly in this way whenever warranted by uncertainties in the foreign-exchange market. Consistent with the return of market confidence, we hope to bring this range down progressively, and interest-rate policy will be closely reviewed with the Fund as part of future programme reviews. We recognise that a sustainable lowering of interest rates will depend on the return of confidence, based on the determined implementation of financial sector restructuring and fiscal consolidation.

9. The monetary programme has been reassessed in light of the larger than expected capital outflows and further depreciation of the exchange rate, which provide clear evidence that the demand for baht-denominated assets has been weaker than originally anticipated. Thus, on the basis of a further rise in the velocity of broad money, M2A is now projected to grow by 1.5 percent by end-1997 and 6.8 percent in 1998. At the same time, the slow return of confidence has increased the demand for currency relative to broad money, and reduced the money multiplier. Therefore, we now aim to contain the expansion of reserve money growth and net domestic assets of the BoT to levels within the original programme limits and indicative targets for these aggregates during 1997-98.

External Sector Policies

10. Although current account adjustment is proceeding rapidly, the capital account is weaker than expected. Overall, we still expect to maintain the gross international reserves of the Bank of Thailand at the originally set levels (at least $23 billion at end-1997, equivalent to about four months of imports). However, to give greater flexibility to reserve and debt management to respond to any risks in projected private capital inflows, we have established new performance criteria for the net international reserves (NIR) of the BoT as well as for external public-sector borrowing, for December 31, 1997 and March 31, 1998. We will continue to review carefully these limits, in the context of the overall financing of the programme, in future programme reviews. We will also consult with the Fund on the utilisation of the new borrowing limits.

11. Looking ahead, we believe that strict implementation of financial sector restructuring (explained below) will help restore market confidence and contain outflows. Also, despite the rollover of forward and swap obligations, we expect that the total of such liabilities would be reduced to about $9 billion by end 1998, which would comprise liquidity-related swaps with onshore banks.

12. It remains our intention to remove as quickly as possible the restrictions on purchases and sales of baht by non-residents as well as the restrictions on baht-denominated borrowing by non-residents, and on the sale of debt instruments and equities for

baht. We expect this will contribute to an early restoration of confidence.

III: Financial Sector Restructuring

13. As envisaged in the original programme, we have made very considerable progress in elaborating the governments's strategy for the overall restructuring of the financial sector (this was done through a comprehensive announcement on October 14, 1997), and in moving decisively toward its implementation (six emergency decrees setting out the legal basis for our strategy have now been ratified by Parliament).

14. As envisaged, we are moving ahead as expeditiously as possible with the restructuring of the 58 suspended finance companies. Box A summarises the key steps in the process: (i) establishment of the full institutional structure in the coming weeks; (ii) the determination by the Financial Restructuring Agency (FRA) of the status of the 58 suspended finance companies by the end of November according to the strongest possible criteria; (iii) the disposal by the FRA of all good assets of closed finance companies as soon as possible thereafter; and (iv) the completion of disposal of all assets by the FRA by the end of 1998. This restructuring will proceed with transparency and without any interference.

15. We have also elaborated the strategy for pre-emptively recapitalising and strengthening the remainder of the financial system, so that its regulatory framework can be brought fully in line with international best practices by the year 2000, and that governance concerns regarding the management of this key sector can be transparently addressed. The BoT will have a clear mandate to carry out the necessary restructuring of the sector. Key steps toward this end include: (i) the early tightening of loan-classification rules and their progressive strengthening over the programme period to reach international best practices by 2000; (ii) timetables for the recapitalisation of all undercapitalised financial institutions during 1998; (iii) streamlining of bankruptcy procedures; and (iv) reaffirmation of disclosure and auditing requirements for all financial institutions.

16. Crucial for both parts of the strategy is the liberalisation of foreign equity investment in the financial sector. Thus, the government has already announced the full liberalisation of such investment for a period of 10 years, with all those who enter in this period being grandfathered permanently with respect to the absolute amount of their equity holding.

IV: Privatisation, Social Services and Legal Framework

17. Privatisation is one of the key medium-term goals of our programme. We have completed the preliminary work needed to increase the role of the private sector in energy, public utilities, communications and transport sectors. We expect to announce firm plans in these areas by June 1998. The majority-owned state enterprises that are

already corporatised will be the first ones to be privatised. Indeed, we intend to reduce the government's stake in the national airline (currently 93 percent) and Bangchak petroleum company (currently 80 percent) to well below 50 percent by mid-1998, if market conditions permit. We also intend to submit to Parliament by June 1998, the necessary legislation to facilitate the privatisation of the state enterprises that are not currently corporatised.

18. Given the sharper-than-expected impact on the domestic economy of the adjustment process, the government is determined to accelerate the implementation of plans to protect the weaker sections of society. Thus, we expect the Asian Development Bank to move speedily and announce a social sector support programme by early 1998. With the help of the World Bank, we hope to widen even further the reach of our social services, and we expect to expand on the above initiatives by the start of the second year of the programme period.

19. The government has also made considerable progress in bringing the legal and regulatory framework in line with international standards and consistent with the smooth implementation of the overall economic programme. Financial sector legislation has already been reviewed and amended as part of the restructuring exercise, we will be amending the Currency Act in order to modernise the regulatory framework for central banking operations; and amendment of the Bankruptcy Law and Civil and Commercial Code are also envisaged to facilitate implementation of the financial restructuring framework.

20. It is our firm belief that the bold and detailed policy measures enunciated here, together with the greater transparency that we have adopted on economic data and policies, will lay the foundation for a decisive turnaround in confidence and economic performance, and lead to a resumption of capital inflows. The government is prepared to take any further measures that may become appropriate for this purpose, will consult with the Fund on the adoption of any such measures, and will provide the Fund with any necessary information in accordance with the policies of the Fund on such consultations.

Sincerely

Tarrin Nimmanhaeminda
Minister of Finance

Chaiyawat Wibulswasdi
Governor, Bank of Thailand

Annex D: Budget Cuts in Thailand

A total of 100 billion baht (U.S. $2, 857 million) was cut from Thailand's 1998 fiscal budget. Following are the areas affected:

	Budget Allocation	Amount Cut	Percent	Final Figure
General Administration	**1194, 979.43**	**21,477.42**	**11.02**	**173,502.02**
State admin.	43,351.08	3,967.81	9.15	39,383.27
Defence	97,255.44	11,514.79	11.84	85,740.66
Internal security	54,372.91	5,994.82	11.03	48,378.09
Community & Social Services	**379,281.74**	**27,489.48**	**7.25**	**351,792.25**
Education	215,720.05	11,484.56	5.32	204,235.49
Public health	69,648.66	7,798.06	11.20	61,860.60
Social welfare	34,433.51	363.12	1.05	34,070.39
Housing & communities	45,791.62	6,661.01	14.55	39,130.61
Religion & culture	13,687.90	1,182.73	8.64	12,505.16
Economic	**262,411.51**	**50,234.04**	**19.14**	**212,177.46**
Fuel & energy	2,277.22	459.64	20.18	1,817.58
Agriculture	71,628.73	9,180.40	12.82	62,448.33
Mineral resources	4,746.80	586.01	12.35	4,160.78
Transport & telecom	151,774.67	35,586.32	23.45	116,188.35
Other economic services	31,984.09	4,421.67	13.82	27,562.42
Other	**86,327.34**	**799.05**	**0.93**	**85,528.28**
Total	**923,000.00**	**100,000.00**	**10.83**	**823,000.00**

Unit: Million baht
Source: *The Bangkok Post*, 15 October, 1997.

Annex E: IMF Stand-By Arrangement with Republic of Korea (Summary of the Economic Program, December 5, 1997)

MACRO-ECONOMIC POLICIES

1. Objectives

The program is intended to narrow the external current account deficit to below 1 percent of GDP in 1998 and 1999, contain inflation at or below 5 percent, and - hoping for an early return of confidence - limit the acceleration in real GDP growth to about 3 percent in 1998, followed by a recovery toward potential in 1999.

2. Monetary Policy and Exchange Rate Policy

■ To demonstrate to markets the authorities' resolve to confront the present crisis, monetary policy will be tightened immediately to restore and sustain calm in the markets and contain the impact of the recent won depreciation on inflation.

■ In line with this policy, the large liquidity injection in recent days has been reversed, and the call rate has been raised from 12 1/2 percent on December 1, 1997 to 21 percent today, and will be raised further in the next few days.

■ Money growth during 1998 will be limited to a rate consistent with containing inflation at 5 percent or less.

■ A flexible exchange rate policy will be maintained, with intervention limited to smoothing operations.

3. Fiscal Policy

■ A tight fiscal policy will be maintained in 1998 to alleviate the burden on monetary policy and to provide for the still uncertain costs of restructuring the financial sector.

■ The cyclical slowdown is projected to worsen the 1998 budget balance of the consolidated central government by about 0.8 percent of GDP. The present estimates of the interest costs of financial sector restructuring is 0.8 percent of GDP. Offsetting measures amounting to about 1.5 percent of GDP will be taken to achieve a minimum budget balance and, preferably, a small surplus. This will be achieved by both revenue and expenditure measures to be determined shortly. These may include, among others:

- increasing VAT coverage and removing exemptions;

- widening the corporate tax base by reducing exemptions and certain tax incentives;

- widening the income tax base by reducing exemptions and deductions;

- increasing excises, luxury taxes, and transportation tax;

- reducing current expenditures particularly support to the corporate sector; and

- reducing low priority capital expenditures.

FINANCIAL SECTOR RESTRUCTURING

1. The following financial sector reform bills submitted to the National Assembly will be passed before the end of the year:

■ A revised Bank of Korea Act, which provides for central bank independence, with price stability as its main mandate.

■ A bill to consolidate supervision of all banks, including specialized banks, merchant banks, securities firms, and insurance companies in an agency with operational and financial autonomy, and with all powers needed to deal effectively with troubled financial institutions.

■ A bill requiring that corporate financial statements be prepared on a consolidated basis and be certified by external auditors.

2. Restructuring and Reform Measures

■ Troubled financial institutions will be closed or if they are deemed viable, restructured and/or recapitalized. The government has already suspended 9 insolvent merchant banks (on December 2, 1997). These banks have been placed under the control of MOFE and required to submit a rehabilitation plan within 30 days. These plans will be assessed in consultation with Fund staff and, if not approved, the institution will have its license revoked.

■ A credible and clearly defined exit strategy will include closures as well as mergers and acquisitions by domestic and foreign institutions, provided the viability of the new groupings is assured. Clear principles on sharing of losses among equity holders and creditors will be established.

■ The disposal of nonperforming loans will be accelerated.

■ The present blanket guarantees which will end in three years will be replaced by a limited deposit insurance scheme.

■ A timetable will be established for all banks to meet or exceed Basle standards.

■ Prudential standards will be upgraded to meet Basle core principles.

■ Any support to financial institutions will be given on strict conditions.

■ All support to financial institutions, other than BOK liquidity credits, will be provided according to pre-established rules, and recorded transparently.

■ Accounting standards and disclosure rules will be strengthened to meet international practice. Financial statements of large financial institutions will be audited by internationally recognized firms.

■ Manpower in the unit supervising merchant banks will be sufficiently increased to make supervision effective and to allow proper handling of troubled banks.

■ The schedule for allowing foreign entry into the domestic financial sector will be accelerated, including allowing foreigners to establish bank subsidiaries and brokerage houses by mid-1998.

■ Borrowing and lending activities of overseas' branches of Korean banks will be closely monitored to ensure that they are sound. Nonviable branches will be closed.

■ BOK's international reserve management will be reviewed with the intention to bring it closer to international practice.

■ Deposits with overseas branches of domestic banks will not be increased further, but gradually withdrawn as circumstances allow. Financial institutions will be encouraged to improve their risk assessment and pricing procedures, and to strengthen loan recovery; actions in these areas will be reviewed as part of prudential supervision.

OTHER STRUCTURAL MEASURES

1. Trade Liberalization

Timetables will be set, in compliance with the WTO commitments, at the time of the first review, to:

- eliminate trade-related subsidies;

- eliminate restrictive import licensing;

- eliminate the import diversification program; and streamline and improve the transparency of the import certification procedures.

2. Capital Account Liberalization

The present timetable for capital account liberalization will be accelerated by taking steps to:

- liberalize foreign investment in the Korean equity market by increasing the ceiling on aggregate ownership from 26 percent to 50 percent by end-1997 and to 55 percent by end-1998. The ceiling on individual foreign ownership will be increased from 7 percent to 50 percent by end-1997.

- effective immediately, for foreign banks seeking to purchase equity in domestic banks in excess of the 4 percent limit requiring supervisory authority approval, the supervisory authority will allow such purchases provided that the acquisitions contribute to the efficiency and soundness of the banking sector; legislation will be submitted to the first special session of the National Assembly to harmonize the Korean regime on equity purchases with OECD practices (with due safeguards against abuse of dominant positions.)

- allow foreign investors to purchase, without restriction, domestic money market instruments.

- allow foreign investment, without restriction, in the domestic corporate bond market.

- further reduce restrictions on foreign direct investment through simplification of procedures.

- eliminate restrictions on foreign borrowings by corporations.

3. Corporate Governance and Corporate Structure

■ Timetable will be set by the time of the first review to improve the transparency of corporate balance sheets, including profit and loss accounts, by enforcing accounting standards in line with generally accepted accounting practices, including through:

- independent external audits,

- full disclosure, and

- provision of consolidated statements for business conglomerates.

■ The commercial orientation of bank lending will be fully respected, and the government will not intervene in bank management and lending decisions. Remaining directed lending will be eliminated immediately. While policy lending (agriculture, small business, etc.) will be maintained, the interest subsidy will be borne by the budget.

■ No government subsidized support or tax privileges will be provided to bail out individual corporations.

■ The "real name" system in financial transactions will be maintained, although with some possible revisions.

■ Measures will be worked out and implemented to reduce the high-debt-to-equity ratio of corporations, and capital markets will be developed to reduce the share of bank financing by corporations (these will be reviewed as part of the first program review).

■ Measures will be worked out and implemented to change the system of mutual guarantees within conglomerates to reduce the risk it involves.

4. Labor Market Reform

■ The capacity of the new employment insurance system will be strengthened to facilitate the redeployment of labor, in parallel with further steps to improve labor market flexibility.

5. Information Provision

■ There will be regular publication of data on foreign exchange reserves, including the composition of reserves and net forward position with a two weeks delay initially. Data on financial institutions, including nonperforming loans, capital adequacy, and ownership structures and affiliations will be published twice a year. Data on short-term external debt will be published quarterly.

Annex F: Investment Restrictions in Emerging Equity Markets *(1995)*

Market	Restrictions on Foreign Investment		Restrictions on Foreign Exchange Movements [b]
	Freedom of Entry[a]	Investment Ceilings (percent)	Repatriation of Income & Principal
Argentina	Free	None	Free
Brazil	Free	49 for common stocks, none for preferred stocks	Free
Chile	Some restrictions	None	After one year
China	Only special classes of shares	None for B and H shares	Free
India	Only authorized (institutional) investors	24 in general	Free
Indonesia	Some restrictions	49 in general	Some restrictions
Korea	Some restrictions	15 in general	Free
Malaysia	Free	None	Free
Mexico	Free	None	Free
Pakistan	Free	None	Free
Philippines	Only through B shares	40 in general and 30 for banks through B shares	Free
Poland	Free	None	Free
Sri Lanka	Some restrictions	49 for banks	Some restrictions
Taiwan (China)	Only authorised Investors	15 in general	Some restrictions
Thailand	Some restrictions	10-49	Free
Venezuela	Some restrictions	None	Some restrictions

a. "Some restrictions" implies that some registration procedures are required to ensure repatriation rights.
b. "Some restrictions" implies that registration or authorization of foreign exchange control authorities is required.
Source: *Emerging Stock Markets Factbook,* IFC, 1996.

Index

Zed titles on Multinational Corporations and Globalisation

Globalisation is the current term used to characterise what is happening in the world economy at the turn of the twentieth century. Integral to this process is the ever more dominant position of very large transnational corporations. Zed Books has published a distinguished list of titles examining these phenomena in all their variety and complexity.

Samir Amin: *Capitalism in the Age of Globalization: The Management of Contemporary Society*

Ricardo Carrere and Larry Lohmann: *Pulping the South: Industrial Tree Plantations and the World Paper Economy*

Michel Chossudovsky: *The Globalisation of World Poverty: Impacts of IMF and World Bank Reforms*

Jacques B. Gelinas: *Freedom from Debt: The Reappropriation of Development through Financial Self-Reliance*

Terence Hopkins and Immanuel Wallerstein et al: *The Age of Transition: Trajectory of the World-System, 1945–2025*

Serge Latouche: *In the Wake of the Affluent Society: An Exploration of Post-Development*

John Madeley: *Big Business, Poor Peoples: The Impact of Transnational Corporations on the World's Poor*

Hans-Peter Martin and Harald Schumann: *The Global Trap: Globalization and the Assault on Prosperity and Democracy*

Stephen Riley: *Stealing from the Poor: Corruption, Development and Poverty in the South*

Harry Shutt: *The Trouble with Capitalism: An Inquiry into the Causes of Global Economic Failure*

Kavaljit Singh: *The Globalisation of Finance: A Citizen's Guide*

Henk Thomas (ed): *Globalization and Third World Trade Unions*

For full details of this list and Zed's other subject and general catalogues, please write to: The Marketing Department, Zed Books, 7 Cynthia Street, London N1 9JF, UK or email Sales@zedbooks.demon.co.uk

Visit our website at: http://www.zedbooks.demon.co.uk

3 5282 00498 4384